PRAISE FOR THE PLANT-BASED FOR LIFE COOKBOOK

"This beautiful book is an invitation to enter the renowned Ann Arbor Vegan Kitchen world and come away with all the tips and skills you need to make healthy eating delicious, too. The recipes are easy to follow; they turn out every time; and they'll win over even the pickiest toddler and stubbornest spouse."

~ VICTORIA MORAN, Author of *Main Street Vegan*, host of the Main Street Vegan Podcast, and director of Main Street Vegan Academy

"Not only does Vicki include delicious recipes and beautiful photos in her new cookbook, she also explains the fundamentals of plant-based living in a way that is easy to understand and relate to. This is a must read for anyone wanting to incorporate more plant-based meals into their lifestyle. I can't wait to start cooking my way through this book."

~ HEATHER McDOUGALL, CEO of The McDougall Program & Dr. McDougall Health & Medical Center

"Vicki shares a wonderful collection of healthy plant-based dishes. This book will set you straight on what to eat and why, truly optimizing key ingredients to make your body and taste buds happy. Her recipes are not just vegan, but oil-free as well... a winning combination for chronic disease prevention – and reversal!"

~ EVELISSE CAPÓ, PharmD, DipACLM, Executive Director of Spanish Programs & Culinary Content, T. Colin Campbell Center for Nutrition Studies

"If you can add just one whole food, plant-based cookbook to your library, make it this one. This book is vibrant, beautiful, and creative. It is jam-packed practical pearls that will move your culinary skills to the next level. The recipes tick all the boxes for nutrition, disease prevention or reversal, and flavor. Whether you are new to the plant-based lifestyle, or are a seasoned vegan, be prepared to be delighted and inspired."

~ BRENDA DAVIS, RD, Plant-based pioneer, speaker, and co-author of *Becoming Vegan* and *Nourish*

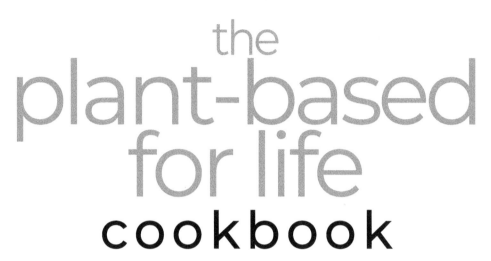

the
plant-based
for life

cookbook

Deliciously Simple Recipes to Nourish, Comfort, Energize and Renew

VICKI BRETT-GACH

Foreword by **Robert Breakey, M.D.**

Published in New York City by the Brooklyn Writers Press,
an imprint of the Brooklyn Writers Co. LLC

www.brooklynwriterspress.com

For information on bulk orders, please email:
contact@brooklynwritersco.com

TITLE: The Plant-Based for Life Cookbook
Deliciously Simple Recipes to Nourish, Comfort, Energize and Renew

ISBN: 978-1-952991-15-8 (e-book)
ISBN: 978-1-952991-04-2 (paperback)
Library of Congress Catalog Card Number: 2021904616

1st Edition

Cover Design by Andy Semnitz

World peace begins in the kitchen.

~Anonymous

To Steve, Sam, and Emily...
for making everything good in the world even better.
I could not have done this without you.

And to my mom...
for showing me how much fun we can have in the kitchen.
Your spirit is always with me.

contents

your health and wellness

This information is intended for educational and informational purposes only and is meant to inspire and motivate you to make empowered choices related to a plant-based vegan lifestyle, health, and wellness. It is not intended to serve as (or to replace) advice from your health care provider.

If you are under the care of a physician, it is understood that it shall be your responsibility to discuss with him or her the merits (and suitability) before embarking upon (or continuing with) a plant-based diet.

You understand too, that you are solely responsible for your self-improvement, and agree to take full responsibility for any consequences that may result from actions you choose to take (or not take) based upon the advice in this book, or upon your understanding of that advice.

foreword .

We are living in unprecedented times.

As we traverse through the worst global pandemic humanity has experienced in over 100 years, we have learned some key lessons. One of the most important is that those who are free from chronic disease and enjoying positive wellness fare much better when they are afflicted with a potentially serious infection like COVID-19. Several studies have shown that the vast majority of deaths from COVID -19 are in people with one or more chronic diseases.

Putting this together with estimates that 70 to 80% of the chronic diseases I see in my office every day — like diabetes, obesity, heart disease, high blood pressure and several cancers — are largely preventable by following some simple lifestyle strategies, we have a clear imperative to change the way we live for the sake of our health, our planet and our children's future.

While genetic factors certainly do play a role, the most important determinants of our overall health, vitality and strength of our immune system are how we eat, move, sleep and manage our stresses on an everyday basis. This is empowering good news for all who are seeking health — but the most common next question I hear is: "How am I supposed to do that?"

As a Lifestyle Family Medicine physician in Ann Arbor, Michigan, I am constantly looking for resources that I can share with my patients to support them in achieving the health and vitality they desire and deserve. I started my own journey on to a plant-based lifestyle in March of 1977, and at that time there was very little support and even fewer resources available to help me learn and understand what constituted optimum human nutrition; let alone the "how to" with respect to making healthy plant-based meals tasty, enjoyable and easy to prepare.

We have come a long way in these last 45 years, and we now find ourselves at the point where there is almost too much information out there — making it hard to find the key references and resources that are truly the best with respect to improving our knowledge of both "the why and the how" of pursuing a plant-based lifestyle.

This is why I consider myself very fortunate to have met and worked with Vicki Brett-Gach over these last 10 years. She is, without a doubt, one of the top plant-based vegan culinary experts anywhere. This book is the culmination of her years of practical experience in both living a plant-based lifestyle, and in teaching others how to do so in a manner that is engaging, fun, tasty, time-saving and nutritious.

You will find that the contents of the book you are now holding will truly support you in charting a path to an amazing experience – a journey that will take you to new levels of health and vitality, while at the same time enjoying the experience of preparing and eating the healthy and delicious meals that you will learn to create in your own kitchen. Enjoy!

Robert Breakey, MD, DipABLM

client testimonials

When I switched to a plant-based lifestyle, I knew it was going to be a healthy choice, but Vicki's recipes have made it an easy and delicious choice! Her recipes for the **Creamy Tomato and Fresh Basil Pasta Sauce (page 171)**, **Simple Blueberry Granola (page 87)** *and* **Indonesian Peanut Sauté (page 178)** are weekly staples in our home. Her recipes for **Creamy Vegetable Lasagna (page 182)** and **Vegan Mac and Cheese Perfection (page 177)** are second to none! Vicki's recipes are so full of flavor you can't help but feel happy and nourished after eating this food!

~SWATI McHALE, Ph.D., *Support Consultant*

I reached out to Vicki because I suffered from IBS issues and wanted to try a vegan diet as management. I knew her cooking would be healthy, but I was so surprised to find that it was also incredibly delicious! After only one week, I experienced a dramatic improvement in my digestion and felt at my best physically and mentally.

~MONICA J. HOLMES, *Data Scientist*

Vicki is a wonderful vegan coach and chef! I've made so much progress with my health since we started working together in 2017. The thing I am happiest about is that my inflammation marker has been cut in half since becoming plant-based. Her recipes have become staples in my kitchen. They are easy and accessible to make, and super yummy!

~MELINDA TOWNS, *Singer and Music Teacher*

I was convinced of the healthfulness of a whole food plant-based diet but just didn't know what to cook for myself. I was tired of trying time-consuming recipes that just didn't taste very good. I was very discouraged. Working with Vicki and cooking her recipes was life-changing for me. Now I'm cooking delicious meals that I truly enjoy. I'm feeling great and my cholesterol levels are finally within a healthy range. Vicki showed me how it's done!

~MARY JO BYRNES, *Homemaker*

I've had a long-standing history with a chronic digestive issue, which was worsening over time. I'd seen specialists throughout the medical community to identify a diet that would help abate the issues by providing alternatives, instead of simply restricting my food options. In early 2018, I had my first all-vegan experience on a fitness retreat, and I was really surprised by how well my body responded and adapted. However, the biggest surprise was the abundance of choices for nutritional alternatives and the deliciousness of all the meals. As soon as I came back from the retreat, I knew for the first time what I needed to do to continue my progress. As such, I sought out a vegan food specialist and I found Vicki.

From our first conversation, I knew Vicki is not only tremendously knowledgeable, but passionate about working to help others find their joy in veganism. Vicki is incredibly personable, understanding, and flexible. With her guidance and support, I discovered a whole new world of food options that I had completely bypassed before. She was indispensable in finding a pathway that worked for me, and for that, I am especially grateful! I wholeheartedly commend her expertise and recommend her services!

~JANET NEICE, *Certified Personal Trainer*

I started my plant-based journey in 2017 after watching the movie What the Health. Prior to that, I was living the Paleo lifestyle, which did not prove to be good for either weight loss or my health. I developed kidney stones and had surgery to remove them.

Upon starting my plant-based journey I had no idea where to begin, what to eat, how to cook, or what to buy. Vicki and I had a series of meetings, a trip to the grocery store, a cooking session in my home, and a pantry cleansing. This was a wonderful way to help me navigate my new lifestyle of plant-based eating. Vicki also has a wonderful website with healthy meals for every part of your day. Her meals are decadent and deliciously healthy.

My journey in plant-based eating has been a challenging one! It has taken me several years to regain my health and I feel amazing. Vicki has been a big part of my health journey.

Vicki helped me realize you do not need to use any oils to sauté ANYTHING. In cutting out oil use for cooking, and eating whole foods, not processed, I can say that at 50 years of age I have never felt better. My energy abounds. I have a plant-based lifestyle to thank for this. Thank you, Vicki, for helping me navigate my way to health and thank you for all your amazing recipes that helped me get here!

~SARAH BOCHENEK, *Registered Nurse*

After watching Forks Over Knives several times, I wanted to eat plant-based. But I knew myself well enough to know I couldn't do it alone. I didn't cook, I didn't pay attention to what I ate, and I had a stressful job that required lots of travel. I wondered how I was going to do this.

I Googled "plant-based eating Ann Arbor" having no idea what I was looking for. Up popped Ann Arbor Vegan Kitchen. Oh my goodness! Here, in my hometown, was a resource to help me begin my plant-based journey. Vicki was Forks Over Knives Plant-Based Certified! I was so excited to find the support I wanted so badly.

I signed up for Vicki's comprehensive three-month coaching program. In those 3 months, I was given the best gift ever; a new healthy lifestyle that continues to this day. Vicki taught me what to eat at home and on the road, how to shop, stock a kitchen with the best tools and ingredients, and most importantly, to love the prep work and the meals I made!

After three years I continue to build on the things Vicki taught me. I've dropped 60 pounds eating great food. Eating plant-based has totally been life-changing for me!

~KIM DOLAN, *Business Consultant*

In March 2017 I went to the emergency room in pain. I was admitted to the hospital with elevated creatine levels. After 24 hours of testing, doctors diagnosed Stage 3 Chronic Kidney Disease (CKD), which likely developed as an effect of the medication I was taking for high blood pressure.

Lose weight, restrict protein intake, limit dairy, don't drink alcohol, drink lots of water.

This was the advice I was given, along with the caution that if the CKD advanced it would mean dialysis or the need for a kidney transplant. Once home I sat, stunned, mentally reviewing everything I heard and experienced at the hospital. Amidst the flurry of advice, someone said, "Try to eat more plant-based protein."

"What?" I asked. "There's a difference between animal and plant protein?"

I grew up in a meat and potatoes household. Seriously... I didn't know that people used more than iceberg lettuce in a salad until I was well into my 20s. So, in that critical moment, I knew that I did not know how to live on a mostly vegetable diet. I said to myself, "What would Oprah do?"

Without hesitation, the answer came. Hire a coach!

Vicki entered my life without judgement, she introduced me to the world of plant-based living. We met at the grocery store where she explained how to prepare some of the vegetables I used to walk by. Vicki showed me how to reorganize my kitchen, how to batch cook, and how to plan ahead so I wouldn't feel hungry.

I joined the Plant-Based Nutrition Support Group and attended small group meetings where members taught me simple skills like pitting an avocado, along with hard to face facts that gave me reason to pause. For instance, why, when my blood pressure was first elevated did no one explain the restorative effects of eating plant protein? Why did I swallow a pill capable of harming my kidneys without fully understanding the risk?

After three weeks of eating a plant-based diet, my blood pressure dropped back to normal and I weaned myself off of medication.

Nine months after giving up animal proteins and enjoying a rich and varied plant-based diet my blood tests improved and my CKD diagnosis was changed from Stage 3 down to Stage 2. The nurse practitioner said that the numbers were in line for "a person [my] age." It was Vicki who first helped me believe that with a change of lifestyle I could improve my diagnosis.

It's been nearly four years since my CKD diagnosis. Instead of seeing it as a burden, I see it as a constant reminder that plants nourish, community supports, and that through the help of a strong and knowledgeable coach, anything is possible.

~Dr. CAM McCOMB, PhD, *Associate Professor of Visual Arts Education*

introduction

Welcome to my kitchen!

I promise that each recipe I'm sharing is delicious and easy to prepare, because these are the same recipes I make at home, demonstrate to my clients, and teach students in our cooking classes.

And I can hardly wait for you to try these in your kitchen too.

Honestly, this is the book I wish I had 12 years ago when I embarked on a plant-based journey. But I've learned that some things just cannot be rushed, because many of these recipes developed through multiple iterations over weeks, months, and sometimes years.

Creating healthy plant-based food is my passion. I love (and I do mean LOVE) this food. But I haven't always been vegan, and I understand how challenging it can be for someone just embarking on this way of eating.

And that's why I'm so glad you're here.

If eating plant-based is new to you, delicious rewards are in store when you prepare this food. Plus, you can likely anticipate improved digestion, enhanced energy, and more happiness.

Yes, happiness. Because you're going to feel better. And sleep better. And be in a better mood more of the time.

Why? You'll be working toward optimal health, with all the lovely trimmings.

Known side effects include improved body weight, heart health, blood pressure, cholesterol, blood glucose levels, and so much more.

So, think of it this way. As you prepare these recipes, you'll be well on your way to not only being healthier and feeling happier, but you'll also be saving the lives of innocent animals and helping to protect and preserve our planet Earth.

Not too bad for starters.

You may already have an inkling that eating this way is a pretty great idea. Let me reassure you.

It is.

Becoming plant-based may be the best decision you've ever made in your life! And I am so excited to share these recipes with you, and for you to see how delicious your life will be.

If you're already a seasoned vegan, thank you so much for joining me. I hope you'll find added inspiration in these pages for even more fun in your healthy kitchen.

One more thing...

Think of this as your personal workbook. Dive right in or explore at your leisure, dog-ear pages, substitute ingredients, scratch notes to yourself, and wipe up spills. If you're reading the e-book version, add notes or consider jotting them down in a dedicated journal - whatever suits you best. Please make these pages your own.

I hope you'll discover favorites that you'll make again and again... ones that will help you (as they have helped me) become Plant-Based for Life.

Warmest vegan wishes,

Vicki

my story

I'm the youngest of three. I was around 11 years-old when my mom was hospitalized, diagnosed with diabetes, and dangerously high blood pressure. As she aged, my mom's struggles became more debilitating. The list became longer with angina, painful neuropathy, kidney disease, and eventually congestive heart failure. Ultimately, she suffered two heart attacks, and finally, a massive stroke in 1997.

Over the years, we all believed (because my mom did) that chronic illnesses were just a normal and unavoidable part of aging. We even thought our mom was a bit of a health nut because she bought skim milk, low-fat cuts of meat, and margarine instead of butter. Back then, I had never heard the word vegan. We had no idea that what our mom was eating was making every one of her conditions worse, and we had no idea that so many chronic illnesses could be avoided, or even reversed, through food.

To this day, I wish I could have shared with her what we now understand to be true about plant-based diets.

family time
After college, I moved to Ann Arbor, Michigan, and a few years later, married my soulmate. We bought our first house and before long, two incredibly beautiful children came along 25 months apart.

post-baby pounds
There I was - a happy, busy mom with two small kids. To my surprise, I noticed for the first time in my life, I had ten stubborn post-baby pounds I couldn't shake.

So, I dieted. For years, I measured portions, counted calories, and kept a food log. Then I tried the Atkins Diet, the one where you can eat the hamburger but not the bun. That was disgusting, and I could not handle it for more than a few days.

Next came the South Beach Diet, and this time I did lose the 10 pounds. But you know what? Instinctively I knew that something was very wrong with any plan that allows you to eat Cool Whip and sugar-free Jell-O, but not fresh fruit.

But I managed to stay on the South Beach Diet for about five months until my misgivings became harder to ignore. I started craving the very healthy, whole ingredients - fruits, beans, potatoes - that South Beach limited, and eventually I knew it was time to liberate my plate from an ideology so flawed. I threw away the artificial sweeteners, the Jell-O, and the Cool Whip, and was ready to find a better solution.

paradigm shift

Although I have always been committed to having healthy habits - I wasn't always working from the best information. When my mother-in-law was diagnosed in 2007 with pancreatic cancer, everything changed. Within only a few months, she was in hospice care.

Nutrition became my focus like never before. I was deeply interested in learning the truth about the connection between what we eat and personal health. That led me straight to The China Study, by T. Colin Campbell, PhD. A new world opened up with an entirely different understanding of the association between animal products and chronic illness.

I continued reading books by plant-based nutrition pioneers, including Dr. John McDougall, Dr. Caldwell Esselstyn, and Dr. Neal Barnard. Inspired by what I was learning, I gave up meat, chicken, and eggs. I completely changed what I was adding to my grocery cart, and what I was serving my loved ones.

Dairy took me a little longer to give up. Only later would I come to understand how addictive dairy products are. If only I had known then all the nondairy strategies I use now to satisfy cravings for creamy sauces, baked goods, and rich ice creams!

joys in the kitchen

When I was younger, I loved helping my mom in the kitchen. Over the years we spent so much time together planning, prepping, cooking, and baking. Those hours are among my most treasured memories.

Naturally, after my husband and I had children, the kitchen became the heart of our family home too. Although I had always loved to cook and bake, once I became vegan,

I loved it even more. Creating in the kitchen, playing with ingredients, and developing new recipes... well, it all had new meaning, and I couldn't get enough of it.

Guess what? Now that I was vegan, I discovered that I had more energy than ever before. My blood pressure fell, and my cholesterol dropped 50 points. And oh yeah, I lost that same 10 pounds again. This time effortlessly, and for good.

Do I measure portions or count calories? Nope. Never.

outreach

I was beyond excited about these discoveries and wanted to find a way to share with others how delicious this food can be. I summoned the courage to ask our local newspaper (The Ann Arbor News) if I could contribute a vegan column to their Food page. To my surprise, they said yes, and later even paid me for it.

Now that I was regularly creating content, photographing food, and sharing recipes, I decided to start my blog, Ann Arbor Vegan Kitchen.

Soon after, I began teaching vegan cooking classes for Whole Foods Market and Washtenaw Community College, and later expanded to teaching privately, semi-privately, remotely, in classroom settings, and to larger groups. Later I was named Co-Director of Culinary Education for the Plant Based Nutrition Support Group (PBNSG.org), where I helped develop their comprehensive plant-based cooking class curriculum.

I am very proud to be a Master-Certified Vegan Lifestyle Coach and Educator as a two-time graduate of Main Street Vegan Academy, and I currently work with clients who need a helping hand as they try to reach their plant-based goals.

I've had the privilege of working with clients across the nation facing almost every imaginable challenge, often a health scare, and I am here to help you, too.

For more information about working together, please visit:
annarborvegankitchen.com

your story

Now it's your turn.

What's YOUR story?

What brings you to this point?

What are you hoping to achieve when you change your diet?

- On a scale of 1 to 10, how important is this goal to you, and how ready are you for this change?

- What doubts or concerns (if any) do you have about moving forward?

- What do you feel might be your biggest obstacle(s) to making this lifestyle work for you?

- Will you have support from family and/or friends?

Let's explore together a few of the concerns I hear most often from people contemplating living a plant-based life. Consider if any of the following concerns resonate with you.

Dairy, Meat & Comfort Foods

"I'll miss my old foods (dairy, meat, etc.) too much."

Let's start with dairy. It's addictive!

Protein fragments (opioid peptides) in dairy, called casomorphins, attach to receptors in the brain, which result in the production of small releases of dopamine. It is not your fault that you crave cheese! The good news is that you can conquer the physical addiction within just a couple of weeks.

And whether it's dairy, meat, or comfort foods (in general), your successful transition to a healthier diet ultimately is all about loving the new food.

So, here's just a smattering of mouth-watering recipes you'll find in these pages to soothe, satisfy, inspire, and comfort, all without accompanying cholesterol, added hormones, or digestive stress.

- Mac and Cheese Perfection (page 177)
- Peanut Butter and Jelly Cookies (page 233)
- Favorite Baked Tempeh Burgers (page 117)
- Creamy Tomato and Fresh Basil Pasta Sauce (page 171)
- Buttermilk Ranch Dressing (page 99)
- Ratatouille Flatbread Pizza (page 122)
- Cream of Broccoli Spinach Soup (page 228)
- Mocha Ice Cream (page 260)
- Pineapple Right-Side-Up Cakes (page 267)
- Moroccan Strawberry Almond Milkshake (page 270)

Time For Meal Prep

"I'm worried meal prep is going to be too time-consuming."

If you don't want to spend a lot of time prepping and cooking, I get it! Here are a few deliciously easy ideas to get you in and out of the kitchen fast.

- Blueberry Peach Overnight Oats (page 53)
- Avo-Curry Toast (page 63)
- Spicy Black Beans and Greens over Rice (page 180)
- Creamy Stuffed Baked Potatoes (page 188)
- Pita Flatbread Pizzas (page 132)

Protein

"How will I get enough protein?"

Without trying, we get all the protein we require by eating a whole food plant-based diet! Nature did the math for us. Plant foods provide all the essential amino acids, which are the protein building blocks our bodies need. And it's a miraculous truth that we don't need to work any harder on getting enough protein than we do with any other macronutrient.

As long as you get enough calories on a whole food plant-based diet you'll be satisfying your protein needs, which it turns out is around 10 to 15 percent of total calories. Even athletes don't need a higher percentage of protein, just more calories.

Whole plant foods that are particularly high in protein include tofu, tempeh, lentils, black beans, chickpeas, quinoa, nuts, and seeds. But all plant foods, even those with lower protein concentrations (think potatoes or bananas) will provide more than enough. Remember, as long as you're getting enough calories on a whole food plant-based diet, you're getting all the protein you need.

The Cost of Eating Plant-Based

"Are these ingredients expensive?"

Which foods create the healthiest and most satisfying meals, per dollar? The answer is a meal made with whole carbohydrates. Satisfying and fiber-rich, whole grains, beans, and starchy vegetables are the very best way to watch pennies as you stretch healthy ingredients into nutritious, delicious meals. Because greens, in particular, provide the most nutrients per calorie, they're the ideal addition. Aim to spend at least 50% of your grocery budget on fresh produce.

Your new best friends in the grocery store:

- *Leafy greens*
- *Other vegetables*
- *Fruits*
- *Whole grains*
- *Beans and legumes*
- *Nuts and seeds*

Support From Family & Friends

"My family and friends don't understand this new way of eating."

It turns out that support can be critical to transitioning successfully to a plant-based lifestyle, so it makes sense that it's one of the most common obstacles people can run up against as they find their footing with this new way of eating.

Yes, it is admittedly ideal to be surrounded by like-minded people when you embark on this journey. But many (and maybe even most of us) do not have that advantage.

Yet even without the support of family and friends, we can make this work together!

How can we make sure others do not get in your way with these new goals? Fortunately, you and only you, have the power to control what goes on your plate.

You are hereby granted all-encompassing permission to be true to yourself. You are hereby allowed to live your truth. And no one shall require that you eat anything you don't want to eat anymore. :)

Happily, there is now an almost endless array of community resources, websites, films, and related material. I've selected some of my favorites that you may want to turn to for extra support. You'll find them in the Additional Resources.

Read and/or listen to these materials anytime, even as daily affirmations. These tools can help remind you why you have chosen to eat well, and why your choices matter.

Try writing in your journal about your dietary successes and any challenges you identify. And please consider me a friend and accountability partner with you in the kitchen, by your side every step of the way.

Each of us is unique. If you have specific questions or concerns or if working together would be helpful for you, please visit my website for more information about customized one-on-one plant-based coaching.

annarborvegankitchen.com

what is a whole food plant-based vegan diet?

This is the gold standard of a healthy lifestyle, and it's centered on lots of whole, unrefined, or minimally processed vegetables, fruits, whole grains, and legumes.

- **Fruit**: apples, bananas, grapes, strawberries, blueberries, oranges, etc.
- **Non-Starchy Vegetables**: lettuce, spinach, broccoli, cauliflower, asparagus, etc.
- **Starchy Vegetables**: potatoes, yams, butternut squash, corn, etc.
- **Whole Grains**: brown rice, whole wheat, barley, quinoa, oats, etc.
- **Legumes**: chickpeas, lentils, black beans, kidney beans, etc.

"...the longest-lived and healthiest people on the planet consume diets based on locally grown starches [i.e., starchy vegetables] and live to the age of 100 at rates ten times higher than the average American!"

-Dr. JOHN McDOUGALL, *The Healthiest Diet on The Planet*

What Is Not Included In A Whole Food Plant-Based Vegan Diet?

Animal products are completely avoided, like beef, chicken, fish, dairy products, and eggs as well as highly refined foods like bleached flour, refined sugar, and added extracted vegetable oils.

What Are The Benefits?

A diet high in animal-based and highly processed foods can make people sick and overweight. But many of these chronic diseases can be prevented, and even reversed by eating a whole food plant-based diet.

A whole food plant-based diet has been shown to:

- lower cholesterol, blood pressure, and blood sugar.

- prevent and often reverse diabetes, obesity, and heart disease.

- improve energy, digestion, and quality of life.

How Do We Get Enough Protein?

No worries. As long as you have enough calories from plant foods, your body will absorb exactly what it needs. Although many of us have been led to believe that only animal-based foods contain enough protein, the reality is that when you eat a whole food plant-based diet comprised of fruit, vegetables, whole grains, and legumes, around 10% of your total calorie intake will be from protein, which is just the amount our bodies need. And consuming too much protein (especially from animal sources) can be harmful to our health in many ways.

Don't We Need Dairy For Calcium?

As with protein, it is not difficult to get enough calcium, you just need to eat whole, plant-based foods. Calcium, like iron, magnesium, and copper, is a mineral found in the soil, where it's absorbed into the roots of plants. It's abundant in many whole plant-based foods, particularly in greens.

Should We Avoid Processed Oils?

Processed oil, like processed sugar, is pressed or extracted from plants. All of the important nutrients, including protein, carbohydrates, vitamins, minerals, fiber, and water, have been left behind. Plus, oil of any kind has more calories per gram than any other food, and excess calories from fat get stored as fat, no matter what type of fat calories you consume. Without any fiber or water in it, oil lacks the properties that signal to our senses how many calories we have eaten, which virtually guarantees we consume more calories than we need or intend. Because oil is highly refined, and its nutritional profile is inferior, eating whole foods such as olives, avocados, and nuts is a better choice than using the oils extracted from those foods. Importantly, processed oils can also harm our blood vessels, and can increase the risk of heart disease, too.

What About B12?

Vitamin B12 is an important and necessary nutrient and experts agree that supplementing Vitamin B12 is required for anyone who eats exclusively a plant-based diet. Although B12 is added to some fortified foods (including plant milks, cereals, and nutritional yeast), it's hard to know how much we're absorbing. Because B12 is crucial for healthy brain function, cognition, our nervous systems, and more, just think of it as an insurance policy, and take a B12 supplement.

Dr. Michael Greger recommends that adults under age 65 take 2,000 mcg each week (or a daily dose of 50 mcg) of Vitamin B12 (cyanocobalamin) and that adults over 65 take at least 3,000 mcg each week.

vegan versus plant-based

Is there a difference between vegan and plant-based?

Yes, there is, but there's lots of overlap too.

Veganism is generally defined by what's avoided. Not harming animals is of primary concern to vegans, so they do not eat meat, poultry, fish, dairy, or eggs, and usually avoid wearing animal products (like leather, wool, fur, and silk), or using products made with (or tested on) animals, including cosmetics, cleansers, or furniture.

Although a vegan diet can be healthy, it isn't always. Why? Because Diet Coke and French fries are vegan, and so are lots of highly processed and refined ingredients, like white sugar and white flour. From a nutritional perspective, these aren't, of course, always the best choices.

Plant-based, on the other hand, typically refers to what is included in the diet, as opposed to what is not. While many people calling themselves "plant-based" do eat exclusively plant foods, others use that term more loosely and still eat eggs, dairy, or fish. Maybe you've seen this yourself when someone orders a Salmon Caesar Salad at a restaurant because salad includes plants.

In other words, some people have gotten confused by the term.

That's why I identify as vegan and plant-based, clarifying that I not only avoid animal products, but I also choose to eat exclusively whole (or minimally processed) plant foods.

Now that you know the difference, you have a choice too.

We know that what we eat today, can (and likely will) impact our future personal health. Will we be glad tomorrow, next week, next month, and next year about what we ate today?

Let's do this together!

Let's choose to reclaim our best energy, achieve vibrant good health, and nourish ourselves (and our loved ones) with the best diet on the planet.

keys to plant-based success

Eat More Real Food

You may find you're eating a larger quantity of food than you expected with a whole food plant-based diet, and maybe even more often. You'll enjoy generous amounts of satisfying starchy vegetables (like potatoes, corn, and butternut squash), whole grains (like brown rich, oats, barley, and quinoa), and legumes (like black beans, lentils, and chickpeas), with plenty of leafy greens and other non-starchy vegetables (like spinach, kale, broccoli, zucchini, and cauliflower), plus delicious fruits like berries, apples, pears, bananas, and oranges. Please have lots of wonderful healthy food, and ONLY wonderful healthy food.

Say No Thank You to Highly Processed Foods

Avoid all added oils, as well as refined sweeteners. Instead of white flour and white rice, look for sprouted whole grain counterparts.

Try Batch Cooking

An important secret to successfully navigating healthy food choices is to ensure you have great options available at all times. Prepare satisfying comfort foods at home to last all week, like beans, soups, and stews.

That's where batch cooking comes in, which simply refers to a system of preparing healthy foods in larger quantities, to ensure there are healthy choices conveniently available, ready and waiting, as we need them.

Why? Because by dinner time, we're hungry! Maybe tired and stressed too. And though we may have the best of intentions to eat whole plant-based foods at every meal, anyone's resolve can be tested after a long hectic day.

By prepping key ingredients and recipes ahead of time, healthy foods will be at your fingertips. That makes this way of eating not only enjoyable, but sustainable, which can make all the difference in your plant-based eating success.

So, unless you're going to be paying someone else to cook for you, you'll want to make batch cooking something of a priority.

Prepare a few meals and/or ingredients you can mix and match throughout the week. Feel free to keep things as simple as you like, for as long as you like.

Which ingredients are the building blocks for your favorite meals? Decide which staple items to prep, and then consider which ones you can make at the same time. For example, maybe you can bake potatoes or sweet potatoes, while you roast butternut squash and onions in the same hot oven. Perhaps you can steam greens in your pressure cooker while you're steaming brown rice in a rice cooker. Maybe while a pot of soup is simmering, you'll be baking breakfast muffins for the week ahead.

Plan a Late-Week Audit

As the week progresses, assess the inventory in your refrigerator. Have you used most of the vegetables, beans, and grains that you prepared? If not, throw leftovers into a pot of soup or dry-sauté ingredients together for sprouted whole grain burritos. Or package up the extras (while still fresh) to store in the freezer for another time.

Keep in mind...

- It takes time to reboot and retrain your palate. Be patient and stick with it.

- You will feel satiety with healthy comfort foods that you prepare at home, like soups, stews, beans, and whole grains.

- Begin each day with steamed or roasted green vegetables as part of (or before) breakfast. Starting with greens in the morning has been proven to reduce sugar cravings later in the day.

- Boldly believe in yourself and your body's ability to be its best if you give it the right conditions to do so.

- Set a daily intention. Planning what you will be eating (to the extent that it's practical) can be a useful tool as you connect the dots between what you are doing and how you are feeling.

- Don't mortgage your health to fit in or let anyone talk you into eating food you don't believe in. You know better than most people around you about the consequences.

- Try not to eat standing up, watching TV, or out of a bag, and eat only food that would get your approval if you were paying attention. Make sure everything you eat is food you really, truly want your system to absorb.

- What matters is what works for YOU! Experiment to find YOUR perfect solutions (which may even change over time, depending on your energy, comfort level, available time, budget, skill set, etc.).

- Be compassionate with yourself. Look for progress, not perfection, as you're building new and wonderful habits.

ways to eat more leafy greens

Leafy green vegetables, cooked or raw, are so jam-packed with powerful health-producing benefits, they've earned the prize for most nutrient-dense food on our planet. Yet, slipping more of these veggie stars into our diets can seem daunting if you are new to greens, or they, to you. How can you get started?

BUY THEM

Write greens on your grocery list every single week.

The first step to eating more greens is to make sure they're handy. Bring home something familiar (like spinach), and then challenge yourself to choose one you haven't ever tried before... maybe kale, escarole, chard, bok choy, or beet greens. Remember that fresh leafy herbs like flat-leaf parsley, basil, and cilantro are loaded with nutritional benefits too, as well as flavor.

SIMPLIFY

Look for pre-washed greens like baby kale, arugula, and collards.

It's a simple convenience, but ready-to-use greens can make all the difference in the world. Look for the ever-growing variety of pre-washed greens in bags and clamshell boxes and buy organic if/when your budget allows.

Buy frozen greens.

Frozen greens are a great value and a nice time-saver too. Already cleaned and prepped, you can always find spinach, and sometimes collards, kale, chard, or mixed leafy greens flash-frozen, so adding a bag to soups and stews is easy as can be.

USE THEM DAILY

Start your morning with a green smoothie.

Add fresh greens to a high-powered blender, along with whatever fresh or frozen fruit you have on hand for a boost so energizing, you'll feel better inside and out.

Add greens to lunchtime wraps.

Midday is the perfect time for greens in a delicious salad sandwich wrap. Spread hummus on the inside of a warm sprouted whole grain tortilla, and add crisp, fresh salad greens. Or, if you have them, add leftovers of steamed greens and rice from dinner the night before.

Make greens at dinnertime non-negotiable.

Add fresh or frozen greens to everything from soups and stews to pastas and stir-fries. Avoid over-cooking greens to keep flavor at its best. Toss greens over veggie burgers or on top of pizza. And of course, enjoy huge dinner salads that include all your favorites.

Step up your game. Try to use greens for breakfast, lunch, and dinner.

Keep greens on your radar at every meal and experiment freely. Some greens have a more assertive, even bitter flavor that might require multiple exposures. I have grown to love greens, but it took time for my palate to adjust. So be patient and persevere as you discover new favorites to love for a healthy lifetime. It is truly worth the effort.

your new vegan pantry

The transition from the old foods to your new selections can be a little challenging, because you may wonder where to begin. First, go through each product in your pantry. Eliminate everything that no longer meets your new requirements.

Next, plan to add back to the pantry a little at a time, as you shop each time over the next several weeks. Eventually, your new pantry will be filled exclusively with ingredients designed to help you reclaim your vibrant good health!

BEANS

Keep a variety of both dried and canned beans on hand. I usually have (at a minimum) dried red lentils, brown lentils, and split peas, plus cans of black beans, kidney beans, and chickpeas. Other nice ones to keep handy: small red beans and navy or pinto beans.

ORGANIC CANNED TOMATOES

Organic Tomato Paste
Organic Tomato Sauce (no sugar, no oil)
Organic Crushed (or Diced) Tomatoes

VEGETABLE BROTH

Keep a few boxes on hand to be ready to add extra flavor to almost any dish. Look for a brand with no added sugar or oil (like ones by Pacific and Trader Joe's).

GRAINS

Keep your pantry stocked with long-grain brown rice, pearled barley, quinoa, rolled old-fashioned oats, and steel-cut oats. Experiment to find other grains you like too, such as bulgur, farro or millet.

PASTA

Whole wheat spaghetti, rotini and penne (or other shapes you like). If you avoid gluten, look for brown rice varieties, or pasta made with lentils, quinoa, etc.

FLOURS (Store in Freezer)

Oat Flour
Almond Meal (or Almond Flour)

BREADS (Store in Freezer)

Sprouted whole grain English muffins, breads, tortillas (like ones made by Food for Life/Ezekiel)

NUTS & SEEDS

Keep raw almonds, cashews, pecans, and walnuts on hand for use in salads, stir-fries, and sauces. Once open, store them in the refrigerator to stay fresh. I also keep ground flaxseed (also called flaxseed meal) on hand and store that in the freezer. (Ground flax when combined with water is a great egg substitute in baking.)

NUT BUTTERS

In the refrigerator, store open jars of raw almond butter and natural peanut butter, for baking or quick snacks.

DRIED FRUITS

Raisins, dried apricots, and dates are great to use in baking. I like dried cherries and cranberries too but use only ones that are unsweetened and without oil, which can be found online.

SWEETENERS (For Baking)

Medjool or Deglet Noor Dates (my favorite dates are made by Date Lady)
Date Lady Date Syrup
Unsweetened Applesauce
Bananas

NONDAIRY MILKS

Almond Milk, unsweetened plain or vanilla
Organic Soy Milk, unsweetened plain

CHOCOLATE

Cocoa or Cacao powder, unsweetened
Vegan Chocolate Chips (optional)
Vegan Semi-sweet Baking Chocolate (optional)

DRIED HERBS & SPICES

Allspice
Apple Pie Spice
Basil
Bay Leaves
Berbere Seasoning
Black Pepper (coarsely ground)
Cayenne Pepper
Chili Powder
Cinnamon
Cajun or Creole Seasoning
Coriander
Cumin
Curry Powder
Dill
Garam Masala
Garlic Powder
Ground Ginger
Harissa Seasoning
Italian Seasoning
Kosher Salt
Nutmeg
Onion Powder
Oregano
Paprika
Pumpkin Pie Spice
Red Pepper Flakes
Smoked Paprika
Smoked Salt
Tarragon
Turmeric
Vanilla (pure vanilla extract or vanilla bean powder)

NUTRITIONAL YEAST

A mildly cheesy flavored, slightly savory ingredient, high in vitamin B12, and often added as an ingredient to sauces or sprinkled over pasta and popcorn.

VINEGARS

Balsamic Vinegars (my favorites are made by California Balsamic)
Raw Organic Apple Cider Vinegar
Rice Vinegar

REFRIGERATED CONDIMENTS

Hummus (oil-free)
Dill Pickles
Mustard(s)
Hot Sauce (my favorite is Choluha)
Bragg Liquid Aminos (a raw, gluten-free soy sauce)
BBQ Sauce without sugar (like Date Lady)
Vegan Worcestershire Sauce
Ketchup without sugar
Miso

OPTIONAL ADDITIONS

Tofu
Tempeh
Kite Hill nondairy cream cheeses and unsweetened plain yogurt
   (made with almonds and water)
Treeline nondairy cheeses
   (made with cashews, probiotics, and water)

For more information about ordering from these companies online:

California Balsamic
californiabalsamic.com

Date Lady
ilovedatelady.com

Food for Life/Ezekiel
foodforlife.com

Kite Hill
kite-hill.com/our-food/cream-cheese-style-spreads

Treeline
treelinecheese.com

equipment essentials

Do yourself a huge favor and gather the right equipment to make your life easier in the kitchen. It makes such a difference! Since people often ask me what I use, where I have personal favorites, I'm sharing what you'd find in my kitchen.

Good Quality Knives

Be sure to collect at least a couple of very good knives that fit your hand well. The right knives will last a lifetime, so think of them as an investment in your health. My favorites are chef's knives and paring knives made by Henckels and Wüsthof. Look for a comfortable grip, balanced feel, and full-tang handle.

Cutting Boards

I use three large cutting boards made by Epicurean. I like how they look and feel, and they're durable, lightweight, dishwasher safe, and eco-friendly.

Large Skillet

My favorite is a large 12-inch Classic Chef's Pan made by Scanpan (with handles on each side) for sautéing onions, making tofu scrambles, and much more. These pans clean up well and are ideal for oil-free cooking.

Nonstick Roasting Pan

I roast vegetables every week in large and small roasting pans made by Scanpan. I use these over and over, for roasting bell peppers, asparagus, butternut squash, onions, cauliflower, sweet potatoes, and more. No matter what caramelizes to the pan, they clean up like a dream.

when your budget allows

Electric Pressure Cooker

My pressure cookers are probably my number one friend in the kitchen for preparing potatoes, bean dishes, soups, chili, and stews. Most brands work well, but I've always been a special fan of the brand Zavor. I've even used up to four of their electric pressure cookers lined up together on the counter at the same time for special events where I've prepared dinners for 40 to 50 people.

High Speed Blender

For me, Vitamix can't be beat for the smoothest hummus, salad dressings, sauces, soups, and much more. I used mine for 10+ years before passing it along to my daughter to use in her first apartment. I replaced it with a new model with more bells and whistles, but any of them (including refurbished ones) will last forever.

Food Processor

I use a large Breville (which I love) for quickly mixing batters, shredding potatoes, and dicing vegetables in large quantities. Additionally, I use a small 3-cup KitchenAid food processor (probably less often) for making quick work of little jobs, like chopping one onion or making breadcrumbs.

Air Fryer

Air frying creates extra crispy results in about half the time a traditional oven would require. It's an exciting kitchen addition for oil-free "fried" potatoes, crispy tofu, and more. I've loved my Philips for several years, and I also love my Breville Air which has a larger capacity.

handy helpers

Salad Spinner
Makes quick work of washing salad greens.

Silicone Brownie-Bites Pan
Makes oil-free baking a delight.

Silicone Muffin Pan
Eliminates the need for parchment baking cups.

Large Mixing Bowl
Comes in handy over and over.

Rice Cooker
My favorite way to make brown rice and quinoa.

Panini Press
For crisping sandwiches and grilling cooked potatoes.

Large Soup Pot
For preparing stovetop soups, sauces, and stews.

Ice Cream Machine
For wonderful plant-based ice creams.

Souper Cubes
In all sizes for freezing leftovers in individual portions.

energizing mornings

blueberry peach overnight oats

Serves: 1

This easy breakfast can make your healthy resolve deliciously sustainable. It's sweet without sugar, and full of health-enhancing fiber and antioxidants.

⅓ cup rolled oats

½ teaspoon cinnamon

unsweetened plain or vanilla almond milk

⅓ cup frozen blueberries

¼ cup frozen peaches, roughly chopped

1 tablespoon raisins

1 tablespoon raw or toasted slivered almonds

Add rolled oats and cinnamon to a small jar. Carefully pour just enough almond milk into the jar to cover oats.

Pack to the top of the jar with frozen fruit, raisins, and almonds. Cover jar tightly and refrigerate overnight (or longer).

tofu power scramble

Serves: 6-8

This nutritious tofu scramble is power-packed with colorful greens, bell peppers, and sweet potatoes, and it's an outstanding way to start your day.

1 onion, diced

1 red bell pepper, diced

2 stalks celery, diced

1 package extra firm tofu, crumbled

2 tablespoons Scramble Seasoning (see below)

dash of extra curry powder, to taste

splash of hot sauce, to taste

splash of Bragg Liquid Aminos or soy sauce, to taste

2 large sweet potatoes, steamed and roughly chopped

2 to 3 cups of fresh baby arugula, kale, or spinach, chopped

kosher salt and coarsely ground black pepper, to taste

Heat a large nonstick skillet over high heat. Add onions and dry sauté until translucent. Sprinkle a little bit of water as needed to prevent sticking to the pan. Add bell pepper and celery and continue to sauté briefly. Add tofu and 2 tablespoons of Scrambler Seasoning. Continue cooking over medium high heat, stirring occasionally until tofu is rich in color and begins to turn golden brown.

Season with an extra sprinkle of curry, hot sauce, and Bragg Liquid Aminos, to taste. Add sweet potatoes and greens and continue to cook just until potatoes are heated through and greens have wilted.

Remove from heat. Season with salt and pepper to taste. Serve hot with sprouted whole grain English muffins.

scramble seasoning

1 cup nutritional yeast flakes

5 ½ tablespoons onion powder

2 tablespoons curry powder

4 teaspoons turmeric

4 teaspoons cumin

4 teaspoons kosher salt (optional)

1 to 2 teaspoons coarsely ground black pepper

Blend all ingredients together and store in a small covered jar to have handy whenever you are ready for a tofu scramble.

fruity green smoothie

Serves 1 or 2

This green smoothie tastes only like the fruit yet provides all the nutritional advantages of greens too. Refreshing and delicious, it's incredibly energizing, and actually makes you feel great inside and out.

1 grapefruit, peeled, sliced in quarters

1 apple, unpeeled, cut in quarters, with the core, seeds, and stem removed

1 banana, peeled, quartered

1 to 2 cups fresh baby kale and spinach

4 to 8 ice cubes

Place all ingredients in a high-powered blender. Process first on low, and gradually work up to high speed until mixture is completely smooth.

Pour into glasses and enjoy immediately.

cinnamon pancakes with blueberry date syrup

Makes 11 or 12 pancakes

These little pancakes are fluffy and tender, gluten-free, flour-free, sugar-free, and oil-free, and topped with a simple fruit syrup of blueberries blended with dates.

2 ripe bananas

2 cups rolled oats

1 cup unsweetened nondairy milk

3 tablespoons date syrup

1 tablespoon pure vanilla extract

1 teaspoon baking powder

1 teaspoon cinnamon

pinch of salt (optional)

Add to a food processor or high-powered blender the bananas, oats, milk, date syrup, vanilla, baking powder, cinnamon, and salt (if using). Blend until smooth.

Heat a large skillet or non-stick griddle over medium high heat.

Pour ¼ cup of batter onto the griddle for each pancake, allowing room between pancakes for flipping. These pancakes cook fast! After about 2 minutes, when small bubbles appear in the center of the pancakes, quickly and carefully flip to other side.

Allow to cook on the second side only about another minute or two, until golden. Remove pancakes from griddle and serve warm with syrup.

blueberry date syrup

1 ½ cups fresh or frozen blueberries

6 tablespoons water

3 Medjool dates, pits removed

Place berries, water, and dates in a high-powered blender and process until smooth. Drizzle over the pancakes or serve on the side. Top with additional fresh berries (if desired).

baked red flannel hash

Serves 6 to 8

This lovely oven-baked hash is full-on comfort food with loads of diced Yukon Gold potatoes, sweet potatoes, onions, and beets. It practically glows with exquisite color and is perfect for a cold winter weekend.

2 ½ pounds Yukon Gold potatoes, scrubbed, unpeeled, and diced in ½-inch cubes

1 pound sweet potatoes, peeled and diced in ½-inch cubes

1 medium sweet onion, diced

½ pound beets, peeled and diced in ½-inch cubes

1 ½ teaspoons kosher salt (or to taste)

½ teaspoon coarsely ground black pepper

¼ to ½ teaspoon Cajun or Creole seasoning

garnish: fresh Italian parsley, chopped (optional)

Preheat oven to 425 degrees. Have ready a large nonstick roasting pan.

Toss all ingredients, except the parsley, together in the pan. Add ¼ cup water to prevent sticking.

Roast uncovered for 20 minutes. Stir gently, and add another splash or two of water, if vegetables begin to look like they are becoming too dry. Continue to roast for another 15 minutes, or until all of the vegetables are tender. At this point, either remove from the oven, or continue to roast for another 10 to 20 minutes, until potatoes brown and crisp a bit more, scraping from the bottom of the pan as needed.

Remove from oven. Garnish with fresh parsley and serve immediately.

avo-curry toast

Serves 1 or 2

Our Avo-Curry Toast (my daughter's name for this) is the easiest answer to savory and satisfying on a weekday morning. My husband loves it so much, he has this at least 3 or 4 times a week.

---

1 or 2 slices sprouted whole grain bread

½ small ripe avocado

juice of ½ fresh lemon

generous sprinkle of curry powder

sprinkle of kosher salt and coarsely ground black pepper, to taste

splash of hot sauce

Toast the bread.

Meanwhile, in a small bowl, mash the avocado. Squeeze fresh lemon juice, and season with curry, salt and pepper. Combine well. Spread avocado mixture on toast, drizzle with hot sauce, and enjoy.

fresh plum and nectarine oatmeal muffins

Makes 12 muffins

Brimming with antioxidant power and fiber, these muffins are great for breakfast, as a snack, or a wonderfully healthy dessert. And they warm up well, so I always try to sneak a few in the freezer too.

2 plums, unpeeled, diced

1 nectarine, unpeeled, diced

4 ripe bananas, mashed

2 cups rolled oats

1 cup unsweetened applesauce

2 tablespoons ground flaxseed meal

2 teaspoons cinnamon

1 ½ teaspoons pure vanilla extract

1 ½ teaspoons fresh lemon juice

1 ½ teaspoons baking powder

½ teaspoon baking soda

Preheat oven to 350 degrees. Line muffin pans with parchment paper liners or have a silicone muffin pan available.

In a large mixing bowl, stir together all ingredients until just combined.

Divide batter evenly into muffin cups, and bake about 25 minutes, or until tops are almost golden and feel just about firm to the touch. Remove muffins from the oven, and place on cooling racks.

Serve warm or at room temperature. Extras freeze well and can be warmed up later in the week.

purple magic baked steel cut oats

Serves 6

As it bakes, the cherries and blueberries make these breakfast oats turn completely purple. One batch is enough for several servings, which will come in handy on busy mornings all week long.

1 cup steel cut oats

1 quart unsweetened plain or vanilla almond milk

1 cup frozen cherries

1 cup frozen blueberries

2 teaspoons cinnamon

Preheat oven to 350 degrees.

Mix all ingredients together in a 9-inch x 13-inch pan. Bake for 50 minutes, until oats are nice and tender.

To serve, top with extra fresh fruit. Cooled leftovers can be refrigerated in a covered container.

panini-pressed potatoes

Serves 1 or 2

---

*Leftover baked potatoes transform into extra crispy oil-free goodness.
Just slice the potatoes in slabs, then season and grill on a panini
press. If you don't have one, just use a grill pan on the stove.*

---

1 or 2 leftover baked russet potatoes

sprinkle of smoked paprika

kosher salt, to taste

optional creamy dipping sauce (see below*)

Heat a panini press.

Slice potatoes length wise. You'll want approximately four long oval slices per potato. Lightly sprinkle one (or both) side(s) with kosher salt and smoked paprika, to taste.

Carefully place seasoned potato slices onto surface of hot panini press. Close lid and allow to grill for 5 minutes or until grill marks are deep golden in color.

Remove from heat and enjoy.

For a creamy dipping sauce, mix together one spoonful of unsweetened nondairy yogurt, a squeeze of yellow mustard and a smidge of smoked salt, each to taste.

double cherry steel cut oats

Serves 4

A cold winter day and hot oatmeal go together like... well, like a cold winter day and hot oatmeal. A pressure cooker makes this extra easy, and sweet and sour cherries add gorgeous color with loads of antioxidants.

1 cup steel cut oats

3 cups unsweetened plain or vanilla almond milk

1 cup frozen tart cherries

1 cup frozen sweet cherries

2 teaspoons cinnamon

1 ½ teaspoons pure vanilla extract

Combine all ingredients in an electric pressure cooker.

Lock lid in place, and seal valve. Select High Pressure with the timer set for 3 to 5 minutes.

After cooking is complete, use either natural release (for thicker oatmeal), or the quick release method (for a chewier bite) to release remainder of the pressure. When valve drops, carefully remove lid.

Serve warm, with additional fresh fruit (if desired).

overnight oats with apples, apricots, and almonds

Serves 1

Throw a few favorite ingredients into a little jar before bedtime. Then just grab and go in the morning. Simply delicious, with no cooking required.

½ cup rolled oats

½ cup apple cider, unsweetened nondairy milk, or water

¼ cup diced apples

1 tablespoon chopped pitted dates

1 tablespoon chopped dried apricots

1 tablespoon dried unsweetened cherries or cranberries

1 tablespoon toasted slivered almonds

½ teaspoon cinnamon, apple pie spice, or pumpkin pie spice

Add rolled oats to a small jar, and carefully pour just enough liquid of your choice into the jar to cover oats. Pack to the top of the jar with fruit, dried fruit, and nuts. Sprinkle with cinnamon or apple pie spice. Cover jar tightly and refrigerate overnight (or longer).

In the morning, empty jar into another bowl, and warm briefly (if desired), and enjoy.

mango blueberry muffins

Makes 12 muffins

Slightly sweet and extra delicious, mango and blueberries are an amazing combination. My kids can devour several of these muffins in one sitting.

4 ripe bananas, mashed

1 cup unsweetened applesauce

2 cups rolled oats

2 tablespoons ground flaxseed meal

2 teaspoons cinnamon

2 teaspoons baking powder

1 ½ teaspoons pure vanilla extract

1 generous cup frozen mango, diced

1 generous cup frozen blueberries

Preheat oven to 350 degrees. Line muffin pans with parchment paper liners or have a silicone muffin pan available.

In a large mixing bowl, stir together all ingredients until just combined.

Divide batter evenly into muffin cups, and bake about 25 minutes, or until tops are almost golden and feel just about firm to the touch. Remove muffins from the oven, and place on cooling racks.

Serve warm or at room temperature. Extras freeze well and can be warmed up later in the week.

super smoothie bowl

Serves 1 or 2

This refreshing Super Smoothie Bowl starts with a base of blended frozen cherries and frozen bananas and is finished with a colorful array of whatever fruits are in season. Try mango, unsweetened coconut, or granola. It's as flexible as you are, and big enough to share.

1 cup frozen cherries

2 frozen bananas

few splashes of water (or juice), as needed to blend

TOPPINGS

fresh fruit (like watermelon, cantaloupe, bananas, blackberries, or raspberries)

nuts (like sliced almonds or chopped walnuts), seeds (like pumpkin seeds) or crunchy granola

Place cherries and frozen banana in a high-powered blender. Process first on low, and gradually work up to high speed until mixture is completely smooth.

Pour into a bowl, flattening the top, and finish with colorful fresh fruit, nuts, seeds, and/or granola and enjoy immediately.

breakfast panini with potatoes and greens

Serves 1

We love paninis at our house, and my favorite is leftover mashed potatoes with steamed greens, but feel free to be creative with your plant-based leftovers. It's all good on a panini.

2 slices sprouted whole grain bread

leftover mashed potatoes*

leftover steamed greens

condiments of choice: spicy mustard, oil-free hummus, hot sauce, or oil-free nondairy cream cheese

Heat either a panini press, or grill pan over medium heat.

Assemble the sandwich. First, spread condiments on each slice of bread (such as mustard, hot sauce, hummus, or nondairy cream cheese). Pile on mashed potatoes and steamed greens.

Sandwich together the two halves, and carefully place onto surface of hot panini press, or skillet.

If using a panini press, close lid, and allow to grill for 5 or 6 minutes. If using a skillet, press down on the top of the sandwich with a large spatula or heavy pan for 2 to 3 minutes per side.

Once sandwich is grilled, remove from heat. Slice panini in half and enjoy.

* Instead of potatoes, feel free to substitute any other leftovers you wish!

mixed berry oatmeal muffin cups

Makes 12 muffins

Made with whole rolled oats and loads of fruit, these muffins are a staple in my kitchen. Somehow the oven transforms this batter into miraculous little muffins, crunchy on the outside, yet soft and chewy on the inside.

4 ripe bananas, mashed

1 cup unsweetened applesauce

2 cups rolled oats

2 tablespoons ground flaxseed meal

1 teaspoon cinnamon

1 ½ teaspoons baking powder

½ teaspoon baking soda

1 ½ teaspoons pure vanilla extract

1 ½ teaspoons apple cider vinegar

2 cups frozen mixed berries

Preheat oven to 350 degrees.

Line muffin pans with parchment paper liners or have a silicone muffin pan available.

In a large mixing bowl, stir together all ingredients until just combined.

Divide batter evenly into muffin cups, and bake about 25 minutes, or until tops are almost golden and feel just about firm to the touch. Remove muffins from the oven, and place on cooling racks.

Serve warm or at room temperature. Extras freeze well and can be warmed up later in the week.

savory veggie bake

Serves 8

Easy, inexpensive, and pantry-friendly, these savory oats cook in broth along with greens and beans, for a breakfast (or even dinner) that's the ultimate in comfort food.

1 Vidalia onion, diced

1 red or green bell pepper, diced

1 clove garlic, minced

4 cups rolled oats

1 15-ounce can chopped fire-roasted tomatoes

1 15-ounce can black beans, rinsed and drained

4 cups vegetable broth

2 to 4 cups baby spinach, roughly chopped

2 teaspoons smoked paprika

1 teaspoon turmeric

1 teaspoon kosher salt (or to taste)

½ teaspoon coarsely ground black pepper

dash of cayenne pepper

½ cup sprouted whole grain breadcrumbs (I make them from Ezekiel bread)

garnish: fresh cilantro (optional)

Preheat oven to 400 degrees.

Have ready a 9-inch x 13-inch ceramic baking pan.

Heat a large nonstick skillet over high heat. Add onions and dry sauté until softened. Sprinkle a little bit of water as needed to prevent sticking to the pan.

Once onions are almost translucent, add bell pepper. Continue cooking over medium-high heat, stirring occasionally until veggies are tender. Add garlic and stir just until fragrant, about 30 to 60 seconds more. Remove pan from heat.

In a large bowl, mix together oats, tomatoes, black beans, and vegetable broth. Add in spinach, all seasonings, and the sautéed veggies. Combine well.

Transfer mixture to the baking dish. Top with breadcrumbs.

Bake uncovered for 40 to 45 minutes.

Garnish (if desired) with fresh cilantro, and hot sauce. Serve hot.

homemade meusli

Makes approximately 2 quarts

*Ready to make your mornings easier than ever? Combine
simple ingredients and refrigerate your treasure in a large jar
or two for the busy week ahead. Breakfast is served.*

3 cups rolled oats

2 cups freeze-dried fruit (my favorite is a mixture of strawberries, mango, and blueberries)

1 cup fruit-sweetened whole grain crisped brown rice cereal, or unsweetened puffed brown rice cereal

1 cup fruit-sweetened whole grain sprouted corn flakes cereal, or unsweetened puffed corn cereal

½ cup organic raisins

½ cup toasted hazelnuts or almonds

In a large bowl, combine all ingredients. That's it!

Store in a glass jar or two and refrigerate to keep fresh.

To serve, top with fresh fruit (if desired) and a splash of nondairy milk.

simple blueberry granola

Makes approximately 1 quart

I love granola, especially this version, without oil or processed sugars. And it's still crispy, crunchy, just sweet enough, and super delicious. It's wonderful sprinkled over oatmeal for a little crunch, tossed with fruit, or mixed into unsweetened nondairy yogurt.

3 cups rolled oats

¼ cup raw walnuts, chopped

¼ cup raw pecans, chopped

¼ cup raw almonds, chopped

1 teaspoon cinnamon

1 cup dates, pits removed

½ cup water

1 tablespoon pure vanilla extract

⅔ cup freeze-dried blueberries

Preheat oven to 325 degrees.

In a large bowl combine oats, walnuts, pecans, almonds, and cinnamon.

Into a high-powered blender, add dates, water, and vanilla. Blend until mixture is quite smooth. Add date paste to the oats mixture, combining well, so that all ingredients are evenly moist.

Spread granola mixture onto a nonstick baking sheet or roasting pan. Bake until golden brown, stirring occasionally, about 25 to 30 minutes. Transfer the baking sheet to a wire rack and allow to cool completely.

Once cool, add in blueberries. Store refrigerated, in an airtight jar.

matcha green tea latte

Serves 1

Matcha tea powder, ground from fine Japanese green tea leaves, has 10 times the antioxidants of regular green tea! Plus, matcha is known to reduce anxiety, inspire mindfulness, create sustained and focused energy, and enhance mood! Good stuff.

---

1 teaspoon matcha green tea powder

1 ½ Medjool dates, or 3 Deglet Noor dates, pits removed

½ cup unsweetened nondairy milk*

½ cup water

Spoon matcha powder into a high-powdered blender. Add dates and milk.

Heat water in an electric kettle or on the stove, until almost boiling. Add hot water to blender.

Blend until all ingredients are completely dissolved, and nice and frothy. Pour into mug and enjoy immediately.

If you have a milk frother, reserve 2 tablespoons of nondairy milk for frothing. Carefully spoon foam over latte before serving.

sensational salads

rainbow harvest salad

Serves 2 to 3

What happens when all of your favorite veggies join forces? Stunning color, amazing nutrition, and out-of-this-world flavor. Use any vegetables you like in your own version, and substitute freely. Roast or steam your veggies for this salad earlier in the day, or even the day before, for easy assembly.

1 to 2 cups fresh salad greens (red or green romaine, baby spinach, baby kale, radicchio, etc.)

½ cup roasted beets

½ cup shredded red cabbage

½ cup sliced grape tomatoes

½ cup sliced raw carrots

½ cup roasted butternut squash

½ cup steamed corn

½ cup steamed shredded Brussels sprouts

½ cup steamed green beans

½ cup roasted asparagus

½ cup steamed beet greens

3 tablespoons oil-free hummus

garnish: raw pistachios, pumpkin seeds, or fresh herbs

dressing: splash of balsamic or flavored vinegar, or freshly squeezed citrus juice

Place a bed of fresh greens at the bottom of a large bowl. Over the greens, arrange the other vegetables in circular fashion, and in order of the rainbow.

Top with hummus. Garnish with your choice of nuts, seeds, or herbs. Dress as desired and enjoy.

vegan kale caesar salad
with polenta croutons

Serves 3 to 4

After becoming vegan, Caesar Salad was probably what I missed the most. But Caesar Salad is back on our menu, and it's better than ever. Traditional romaine gets a colorful makeover with the addition of tender baby kale and crunchy red cabbage shreds, finished with crushed pistachios, pecans, and crispy polenta croutons, and topped with a totally crave-worthy dressing.

6 cups baby kale, chopped

6 cups romaine lettuce, chopped

1 cup shredded red cabbage

½ cup raw cashews

½ cup water

2 tablespoons fresh lemon juice

2 teaspoons brown mustard

¼ teaspoon cayenne pepper

¼ teaspoon onion powder

¼ teaspoon kosher salt (or to taste)

⅛ teaspoon garlic powder

garnish: raw pistachios and/or pecans, crushed

topping: Polenta Croutons (see below)

Place baby kale, romaine lettuce, and shredded red cabbage in a large bowl, and set aside.

Prepare polenta croutons (see right) and set aside.

While croutons are baking, prepare the dressing. Add cashews, water, lemon juice, brown mustard, cayenne, onion powder, garlic powder, and salt into a high-powered blender, and process until smooth.

Toss the salad with desired amount of dressing and refrigerate the remainder.

Garnish with crushed pistachios and/or pecans, top with polenta croutons, and serve immediately.

polenta croutons

homemade or prepared polenta, room temperature and cut into ½-inch cubes

sprinkle of kosher salt (optional)

sprinkle of coarsely ground black pepper

sprinkle of Cajun or Creole seasoning

Into a large bowl, toss polenta cubes with seasonings until evenly coated. Bake either in an air fryer or traditional oven.

AIR FRYER METHOD

Place polenta cubes in the basket of an air fryer in a single layer. Set temperature to 400 degrees and bake for 10 to 12 minutes, or until nice and crispy. Remove from air fryer and set aside.

TRADITIONAL OVEN METHOD

Preheat oven to 425 degrees. Line a large baking sheet with a silicone baking mat or parchment paper. Toss cubes onto prepared baking sheet and bake for 20 to 25 minutes, or until polenta cubes are nice and crispy. Remove from oven and set aside.

fresh corn, tomato, and avocado salad

Serves 4

Not only is this recipe super easy, it's super delicious, with iconic flavors, creamy avocado, and aromatic basil. Save time by steaming the corn the night before and refrigerating overnight to make this salad the next day. Double or triple this for a larger crowd.

2 cups organic corn (2 or 3 ears fresh corn on cob, OR one 10-ounce package frozen corn)

½ cup grape tomatoes, halved

1 tablespoon balsamic vinegar (or to taste)

½ teaspoon kosher salt (or to taste)

¼ teaspoon coarsely ground black pepper

1 ripe Hass avocado, chopped or diced

¼ cup fresh basil, minced (optional)

Prepare the corn, steaming until tender crisp. Remove from heat. Drain, and allow the corn to cool.

Carefully remove kernels from the cob into a bowl with a sharp knife. You'll be able to skip this step if using frozen corn. The cooked corn can be thoroughly chilled in the refrigerator at this point, until ready to assemble.

When ready to serve, in a medium size bowl, toss the corn with the tomatoes and balsamic vinegar. Season with salt and pepper. Mix well. Add avocado and basil (if using). Toss gently and serve immediately.

simple salad with radicchio, hazelnuts, and buttermilk ranch dressing

Serves 4 to 6

This creamy dressing is an all-time favorite at our house and will turn any fresh vegetable combination into a fabulous salad.

1 head radicchio, chopped

1 head romaine lettuce (or leaf lettuce), chopped

BUTTERMILK RANCH DRESSING

1 cup raw cashews

½ cup unsweetened soy milk

½ cup water

3 tablespoons fresh lemon juice

2 teaspoons brown mustard

1 teaspoon balsamic vinegar

¾ teaspoon kosher salt (or to taste)

garnish: toasted hazelnuts

Place salad greens in medium size bowl and set aside.

To make Buttermilk Ranch Dressing, place cashews, soy milk, water, lemon juice, mustard, vinegar, and salt in a high-powered blender, and process until smooth.

Toss salad with desired amount of dressing and refrigerate the remainder.

Top salad with toasted hazelnuts and serve immediately.

arugula and roasted beet salad with cream cheese, dates, and pistachios

Serves 1

This salad is sweet and salty, bitter and acidic, and crunchy and creamy. It's a festival of color, a riot of flavor, and beyond delicious. It actually helped me learn to love beets. See if it makes a believer out of you, too.

1 ½ cups fresh arugula leaves, roughly chopped

⅓ cup roasted beets (red or/and yellow), chopped

1 ½ tablespoons nondairy cream cheese

1 pitted Medjool date, minced

5 raw or dry roasted pistachios, chopped

balsamic vinegar

Onto a plate, spread the arugula. Add chopped beets. Dot the top with cream cheese. Top with minced dates and pistachios. Add a drizzle of balsamic vinegar and enjoy.

summer red-skinned potato salad

Serves 6

This potato salad is a favorite, even with family members who don't like potato salad. That's when you know you have a winner. The flavorful difference comes from fresh herbs and dill pickles, and an amazing dressing that steals the show.

4 cups red-skinned potatoes, scrubbed and cubed

1 cup celery, diced

2 tablespoons dill pickles, minced

2 tablespoons fresh dill, minced (or 2 teaspoons dried dill)

1 ½ teaspoons fresh tarragon, minced (or ½ teaspoon dried tarragon)

CREAMY DRESSING

½ cup raw cashews

6 tablespoons water

2 tablespoons, plus ¾ teaspoon rice vinegar

1 ½ teaspoons fresh lemon juice

1 ½ tablespoons Dijon mustard

1 ½ teaspoons, plus ⅛ teaspoon kosher salt (or to taste)

¼ teaspoon coarsely ground black pepper

Place potatoes in a large pot with cold salted water. Bring to a boil, reduce heat, and cover. Simmer until tender, then drain, and allow potatoes to cool for about 20 minutes more.

Once the potatoes have cooled, place them in a large bowl. Add celery, pickles, dill, and tarragon, and toss together.

To make the dressing, add cashews, water, vinegar, mustard, lemon juice, salt, and pepper to a high-powered blender. Process on low, then gradually work up to high speed until mixture is completely smooth.

Pour dressing over the salad ingredients and combine well. Serve immediately or refrigerate and serve chilled.

red cabbage and mango slaw

Serves 8 to 10

Red cabbage, crispy carrots, delicate cilantro, and sweet mango become a glorious flavor celebration with a light, tangy lime and balsamic finish.

4 cups red cabbage, shredded

4 carrots, peeled and chopped or shredded

2 mangos, diced

¾ cup fresh cilantro, chopped (or to taste)

juice of 1 large lime, freshly squeezed

splashes of balsamic vinegar (to taste)

sprinkle of kosher salt (optional)

In a large bowl, mix together both kinds of cabbage, carrots, mangos, and cilantro. Add lime juice, balsamic vinegar, and salt (if using), and toss completely. Taste for seasonings and adjust as needed.

Allow slaw to chill completely and mix again very well just before serving.

sweet and creamy cabbage and apple slaw

Serves 6 to 8

This slaw is sweetened slightly with apples, with an addictively sweet and creamy dressing made with raisins and cashews.

SLAW

2 cups green cabbage, shredded

2 cups red cabbage, shredded

2 crisp apples, peeled and diced

2 carrots, peeled and shredded

DRESSING

½ cup water

⅓ cup raw cashews

⅓ cup raisins, packed

2 tablespoons brown mustard

2 tablespoons balsamic vinegar

sprinkle of kosher salt (optional)

In a large bowl, mix together cabbage, apples, and carrots. Set aside.

Into a high-powered blender, add water, cashews, raisins, brown mustard, vinegar, and a sprinkle of salt. Process until smooth.

Pour dressing over coleslaw and toss together well. Cover and refrigerate until serving time. Toss well again just before serving.

salad-in-a-jar

Serves 1 or 2

Adding more color and a few nontraditional ingredients keeps big salads interesting, and with an infinite variety of flavor combinations you can create a brand-new version every day.

splash of balsamic vinegar or oil-free dressing of your choice

chickpeas or kidney beans, rinsed and drained

red cabbage or baby kale

green romaine or red leaf lettuce

red or green bell pepper

corn

baby cucumbers or celery

carrots

roasted or pickled beets or fresh tomatoes

mild pickled peppers

baby spinach

olives or baked tofu

walnuts or almonds

raisins or currants

Although these salad ingredients are delicious suggestions, substitute freely with layers of your colorful favorites, sliced, diced, or shredded to fill one quart-size jar.

Start with a clean 1-quart-size wide-mouth glass jar with a lid.

Pour vinegar or dressing into the bottom of the jar.

Slice, dice, or shred ingredients into bite size pieces, as needed. Layer the most sturdy salad ingredients into your first jar first. Add layers of lettuces and other colorful vegetables of your choice, packing all ingredients well, to reduce the amount of air and ensure freshness. Top your salad with the lightest, most delicate ingredients. Close jar tightly with lid.

Keep jar refrigerated until lunchtime.

To serve, pour the entire salad into a large bowl. Or, if preferred, simply turn jar upside down, shake vigorously until dressing is evenly distributed, and enjoy salad directly from the jar.

air-fried bbq tempeh salad with beet caesar dressing

Serves 4 to 6

The combination of crispy greens, BBQ Tempeh, and an amazing dressing creates an explosion of flavor, crunch, and creamy goodness. Outstanding with steamed Brussels sprouts tossed over the top too.

12 cups romaine lettuce, chopped (or salad greens and vegetables or your choice)

BBQ Tempeh (see below)

Beet Caesar Dressing (see next page)

Place salad greens in a large bowl and set aside.

Prepare BBQ Tempeh (see below).

While tempeh is baking, prepare Beet Caesar Dressing (see next page).

Top chilled greens with hot BBQ Tempeh. Drizzle salad with desired amount of Beet Caesar Dressing and refrigerate remainder. Serve immediately.

bbq tempeh

1 8-ounce block tempeh

¼ cup Date Lady BBQ Sauce (or other BBQ sauce sweetened without sugar)

2 tablespoons California Balsamic 7-Herb Italian Balsamic Vinegar (or other balsamic flavor of your choice)

splash of hot sauce

dash of yellow mustard

pinch of kosher salt and coarsely ground black pepper (optional)

Slice tempeh crosswise into 16 slices. Slice again in the other direction, dividing each slice into 4 smaller pieces.

In a flat dish, stir together the marinade: BBQ sauce, vinegar, hot sauce, mustard and salt and pepper (if using). Add tempeh "cubes" and toss until evenly coated with sauce.

AIR FRYER METHOD

Reserving as much of the sauce as you can, carefully place tempeh pieces in the basket of air fryer in a single layer. You will be saving and using the reserved sauce once air frying is complete. (Note that extra sauce inside of the air fryer just tends to burn.)

Set temperature to 400 degrees and bake for 12 minutes, or until deeply golden and crispy. Remove from air fryer and toss tempeh into the dish of reserved sauce. Coat each piece of tempeh with the sauce well and serve immediately.

TRADITIONAL OVEN METHOD

Preheat oven to 425 degrees. Line a large baking sheet with a silicone baking mat or parchment paper. Reserving as much of the sauce as you can, carefully place tempeh pieces onto prepared baking sheet. You will be saving and using the reserved sauce once oven baking is complete. (Note that extra sauce in the oven just tends to burn.)

Bake for about 20-25 minutes, or until deeply golden and crispy. Remove from oven and toss tempeh into the dish of reserved sauce. Coat each piece of tempeh with the sauce well and serve immediately.

beet caesar dressing

½ cup raw cashews

½ cup water

1 small roasted beet (about 1 ¼ ounces)

2 tablespoons fresh lemon juice

2 teaspoons brown mustard

¼ teaspoon cayenne pepper

¼ teaspoon onion powder

¼ teaspoon kosher salt (or to taste)

⅛ teaspoon garlic powder

To prepare dressing, add cashews, water, beet, lemon juice, brown mustard, cayenne, onion powder, salt, and garlic powder into a high-powered blender, and process until smooth.

burgers, wraps and more

favorite baked tempeh burgers

Makes 6 burgers

These tempeh burgers are good enough for special occasions, yet they require such minimal effort. Top with roasted vegetables or simple avocado slices for a lovely finishing touch.

1 clove garlic

1 8-ounce block tempeh

1 onion, roughly chopped

¼ cup ground flaxseed meal

3 tablespoons balsamic vinegar

1 ½ tablespoons Bragg Liquid Aminos or soy sauce

1 tablespoon yellow mustard

generous sprinkle Cajun or Creole seasoning

Preheat oven to 400 degrees.

Add garlic to the bowl of a large food processor and mince briefly. Remove processor lid and add the rest of the ingredients. Process until almost (but not entirely) smooth.

Empty contents onto a clean cutting board. Divide mixture evenly into 6 portions, and form into evenly shaped burger patties. Place burgers on a nonstick baking sheet or oven-safe griddle. Bake for approximately 18 minutes, and carefully flip. Continue baking for an additional 7 minutes, or until golden brown.

Remove tempeh burgers from oven and serve immediately on toasted sprouted whole grain English muffins, along with your favorite flavorful toppings and condiments.

salad wraps with beans and greens

Serves 1

Mix and match with diced avocados, olives, tomatoes, green onions, zucchini, and corn for a new lunch creation, any day of the week. With protein, fiber, minerals and vitamins, a fresh salad wrap like this will keep you energized and focused all afternoon.

1 large sprouted whole grain tortilla

oil-free hummus

⅔ cup fresh spinach leaves, chopped (or other salad greens)

4 spears asparagus, sautéed

½ cup Spiced Beans, Peppers, and Onions (see below)

Spread the tortilla with a layer of hummus. Cover most of the hummus with the spinach, from one side all the way across to the other. Add the asparagus down the center.

Spoon Spiced Beans, Peppers, and Onions mixture over the top. Carefully roll the tortilla as tightly as you can. Slice the wrap into halves or quarters and serve immediately.

spiced beans, peppers, and onions

1 onion, diced

1 green pepper, chopped

1 15-ounce can black beans, rinsed and drained

1 tablespoon Mexican seasoning

Steam-sauté onion and green pepper in a hot pan until tender. Add beans and seasoning, and continue to cook together until well combined, and heated through.

Place a generous scoop or two (approximately ½ cup) in wrap above. Store remainder in the refrigerator.

fabulous beet burgers

Makes 8 to 10 burgers

Beets are incredibly nutritious, and this is a fantastic way to enjoy this powerful superfood. The color is spectacular, and the flavor is outstanding. Serve these open-faced on toasted whole grain buns with your favorite fresh toppings.

3 small (or 2 medium) roasted beets (see below)

1 large roasted onion (see below)

1 cup cooked brown rice, mixed with steamed greens (see right)

1 15-ounce can black beans, rinsed and drained

¼ cup balsamic vinegar

⅓ cup ground flaxseed meal

1 teaspoon kosher salt (or to taste)

½ teaspoon cumin

½ teaspoon Cajun or Creole seasoning

Preheat oven to 425 degrees.

In a large food processor, add the beets, onion, and all other ingredients, and process until almost (but not entirely) smooth.

Empty contents into a color-safe bowl, or onto a clean color-safe surface. Divide mixture evenly into 8 to 10 portions. Form each one into a flattened burger-shaped patty. Place burgers on a nonstick baking sheet or oven-safe griddle.

Bake for approximately 25 minutes, or until almost firm to the touch. Remove beet burgers from oven, and serve on toasted whole grain buns, along with your favorite condiments and toppings (lettuce, tomato, avocado, pickles, mustard, hummus, etc.).

TO ROAST BEETS AND ONION

Preheat oven to 350 degrees.

Wash and trim beets. Trim and peel the onion. Place the beets and the onion into a covered baking dish or wrap each one individually in aluminum foil.

Place the covered baking dish or the foil packets in the oven and roast for one hour. Remove from oven and allow to cool, without opening. Roasting can be completed early in the day, or even the day before. If making ahead, refrigerate cooled vegetables until ready to use.

Once the beets (and onion) have cooled, carefully remove, and discard the thin outer skin from the beets.

BROWN RICE AND STEAMED GREENS

For convenience, cook the greens along with your rice. The amount of greens you use is up to you!

Just wash and chop your choice of fresh greens (beet greens or kale both work great). Add uncooked greens to the uncooked rice and allow both to steam together on the stove or in a rice cooker. This combination is optional. Plain cooked brown rice is fine, too.

ratatouille flatbread pizza

Serves 1 or 2

*Ratatouille is a traditional French vegetable sauté that originated in
Nice. Aromatic, light, and fresh, it's wonderful with (and over) just about
everything. These pizzas are so good, I can eat two at one time.*

2 sprouted whole grain tortillas

1 ½ cups mashed potatoes (my
method is below)

1 ½ cups Ratatouille (recipe to right)

garnish: fresh basil, finely chopped

Preheat oven (or toaster oven) to 400 degrees.

Place whole grain tortillas or flatbreads onto a baking sheet. Slather with a thick
layer of mashed potatoes.

Top mashed potatoes with the ratatouille, and sprinkle fresh basil on top.

Bake flatbread pizzas for approximately 10 to 12 minutes, or until the edges begin
to turn crispy and golden brown, and the center is hot and bubbling. Remove from
oven, garnish with fresh basil, and serve hot.

mashed potatoes

2 Yukon Gold potatoes

unsweetened soy milk

dash of onion powder

kosher salt and coarsely ground black
pepper, to taste

To make mashed potatoes, peel, and chop potatoes. Place them in a pot of water
and bring to a boil. Cover, reduce heat, and continue to simmer until tender. Drain
potatoes, and mash until creamy with soy milk and seasonings, to taste. Set aside
to use over Ratatouille Flatbread Pizza.

ratatouille

1 onion, chopped

1 clove garlic, minced

2 to 3 zucchinis, quartered lengthwise, and thinly sliced

1 red bell pepper, chopped

1 15-ounce can diced fire-roasted tomatoes

1 or 2 pinches of cayenne pepper

handful of fresh basil

kosher salt and coarsely ground black pepper, to taste

Preheat oven to 400 degrees.

Add onions, garlic, zucchini, and bell peppers to a large nonstick roasting pan. Add a bit of water to avoid sticking to the pan, and roast vegetables for about 30 to 50 minutes, or until completely tender, stirring and scraping up any sticking vegetables a couple of times during roasting.

Once vegetables are golden and fork-tender, mix in the tomatoes and cayenne pepper, and toss gently to combine. Continue roasting for another 10 or 15 minutes. Remove from oven. Season with salt and pepper to taste.

Set aside to use over Ratatouille Flatbread Pizza.

grand slam tempeh burgers with spinach and sweet potatoes

Makes 10 to 12 burgers

This burger is full of hearty tempeh, greens, and sweet potatoes, and packed with phytonutrients, complex carbohydrates, and plant-based protein for the win! It's deliciously simple and oven-baked to perfection.

1 8-ounce block tempeh

1 small onion, roughly chopped

2 cups baby spinach

1 medium steamed sweet potato (about 1 ½ cups), peeled and roughly chopped

⅓ cup ground flaxseed meal

¼ cup balsamic vinegar

generous sprinkle of Cajun or Creole seasoning

generous sprinkle of kosher salt (or to taste)

Preheat oven to 425 degrees.

Add all the ingredients into a food processor and process until almost (but not entirely) smooth. Empty contents onto a clean cutting board. Divide mixture evenly into 10 to 12 portions. Form each portion into a flat burger-shaped patty. Place burgers on a nonstick baking sheet or oven-safe griddle. Bake for approximately 25 to 35 minutes, or until golden and almost firm.

Remove tempeh burgers from oven and serve immediately on toasted sprouted whole grain English muffins, along with your favorite flavorful toppings and condiments.

summer rolls with spicy peanut tofu

Serves 1 or 2

Unlike fried spring rolls, summer rolls are generally made with fresh ingredients, and served at room temperature. In this version, I'm adding a spicy sautéed tofu. Be forewarned that these are practically addictive.

2 brown rice spring roll wrappers

⅔ cup fresh spinach leaves or other salad greens

1 medium carrot, trimmed, peeled, cut into matchsticks

2-inch wedge of English cucumber, cut into matchsticks

½ cup Spicy Peanut Tofu (see recipe below)

Follow package directions to prepare rice paper wraps, carefully dipping (one at a time) into a bowl of warm water to get wet, then placing it on a clean cutting board. Working quickly, place spinach leaves evenly over the top, leaving a border of an inch for wrapping. Add other vegetables in a line across the center. Top with Spicy Peanut Tofu.

Gently roll tightly from one side to the other, carefully tucking in the ends as you go, just like a burrito, and serve.

spicy peanut tofu

1 package extra firm tofu, crumbled

¼ cup Bragg Liquid Aminos or soy sauce

¼ cup hot sauce

2 tablespoons natural peanut butter

1 tablespoon balsamic vinegar

Heat a large nonstick wok or skillet, and add tofu to the pan. Brown slightly, stirring occasionally. If needed, add a little water to prevent sticking to the pan. Sprinkle with Bragg Liquid Aminos and hot sauce. Continue to cook until slightly browned. Add peanut butter and balsamic vinegar, and continue sautéing until golden and crispy. Turn off heat and set aside.

oven-baked falafel burgers

Makes 9 burgers

Truly delicious for a casual weeknight meal, with flavors of falafel and the ease of a burger. I like to serve these open-faced on toasted Ezekiel English muffins, topped with hummus, mustard and pickles.

---

2 14-ounce cans chickpeas, rinsed and drained

1 large onion, diced

2 cloves garlic, minced

1 generous cup fresh flat-leaf parsley, densely packed

½ cup rolled oats

3 tablespoons tahini

2 tablespoons hot sauce

3 tablespoons water

2 ¼ teaspoons cumin

2 teaspoons coriander

1 teaspoon salt (or to taste)

¼ teaspoon coarsely ground black pepper

Preheat oven to 400 degrees.

Using a nonstick roasting pan, roast chickpeas, onion, and garlic in the oven for 45 to 50 minutes. Add a splash of water and stir occasionally to avoid sticking. Once the ingredients are golden, remove pan from oven, and set aside.

Turn oven temperature down to 375 degrees.

Into the bowl of a large food processor add all falafel ingredients (including roasted chickpeas, onions, and garlic) and process until almost smooth, and batter begins to stick to itself. Add an additional splash of water, if needed. Remove bowl and blade from base. Form falafel mixture into evenly shaped patties and place them on a nonstick baking sheet or oven-safe griddle.

Bake at 375 degrees for 20 minutes. Flip burgers and bake for another 5 minutes, or until nice and crispy. Remove from oven and serve immediately on sprouted whole grain English muffins along with favorite toppings (tomato, pickles, yogurt, mustard, hummus, etc.).

perfect chickpea salad sandwich

Serves 4 to 6

This chickpea salad is crunchy, creamy, and colorful, and terrific topped with fresh spinach, thinly sliced English cucumbers, and ripe tomatoes. Simple to prepare, and very portable. This one gets a thumbs-up even from our non-vegan friends.

1 15-ounce can chickpeas, rinsed and drained

2 stalks celery, finely chopped

⅓ cup red bell pepper, finely chopped

⅓ cup dill pickles, finely chopped

¼ cup oil-free hummus

1 ½ teaspoons yellow mustard

1 tablespoon fresh dill, minced (or 1 teaspoon dried dill)

handful of fresh Italian parsley, minced (approximately ¼ cup)

juice of 1 fresh lemon (3 to 4 tablespoons)

¼ teaspoon kosher salt (or to taste)

coarsely ground black pepper

whole grain pita flatbreads, or toasted sprouted whole grain English muffins

In a large bowl, mash the chickpeas with a potato masher until flaky in texture.

Add the celery, bell pepper, pickles, hummus, mustard, dill, parsley, and lemon juice. Mix well. Sprinkle with salt and pepper, adjusting seasoning to taste.

Serve on toasted sprouted whole grain English muffins, or in whole grain pita bread pockets.

pita flatbread pizzas

Serves 4

The key to fabulous vegan pizza is loads and loads of fresh toppings and contrasting flavors. Nothing needs to be measured. My favorites are roasted sweet onions, red bell peppers, diced zucchini, crushed pineapple, and ribbons of fresh basil.

---

4 large whole wheat pita flatbreads

pasta sauce, pizza sauce, or tomato sauce (no sugar, no oil)

red bell peppers, diced, and roasted or sautéed

Vidalia onions, diced, and roasted or sautéed

zucchini, diced, and roasted or sautéed

crushed pineapple, drained

ribbons of fresh basil

Italian seasoning (optional)

kosher salt and coarsely ground black pepper, to taste

To serve: nutritional yeast or red pepper flakes (optional)

Preheat oven (or toaster oven) to 425 or 450 degrees.

Slice pita flatbreads in half, and place pita halves onto a baking sheet. Slather with a thick layer of pasta sauce.

Top sauce generously with all the toppings of your choice. Sprinkle the pizzas with a touch of salt and pepper and/or Italian seasoning. Bake for approximately 10 to 12 minutes, or until the edges begin to turn crispy and golden brown, and the center is hot and bubbling.

Remove from oven. Top with nutritional yeast or red pepper flakes (if desired) and serve hot.

plant-happy sides

air-fried onion rings

Serves 4

These onion rings have a crunchy breadcrumb base that starts with either Ezekiel Cereal transformed into seasoned crumbs, or Organic Chickpea Crumbs, which are gluten-free. Both are available either online or at your local grocery store.

1 large Vidalia onion

BATTER

⅔ cup unsweetened soy milk

½ cup oat flour

½ teaspoon paprika

½ teaspoon kosher salt (or to taste)

¼ teaspoon turmeric

DRY CRUMB MIXTURE

1 cup either Ezekiel Original Sprouted Cereal or Organic Chickpea Crumbs (or a combination)

½ teaspoon paprika

¼ teaspoon kosher salt (or to taste)

¼ teaspoon turmeric

Slice off the ends of the onion and remove outer skin. Carefully slice onion into ¼ to ½-inch slices. Separate the rings of the onion from each other to prepare for dipping and set aside.

In a medium bowl, mix the Batter ingredients together.

In a high-powered blender, turn Ezekiel cereal into finer crumbs. If using the chickpea crumbs, you can skip this step.

Pour crumbs into a separate medium bowl and mix in the rest of the Dry Crumb Mixture ingredients. Using separate hands for the wet and dry, dip one ring at a time, first into the wet batter, then into the dry mixture, coating each with crumbs.

Place several coated onion rings in the basket of your air fryer. Try to avoid overcrowding, or they might all stick together.

Bake at 400 degrees, in batches (depending on size of your machine), for about 9 minutes per batch, or until golden and crispy. Repeat batches as needed to use all the onions and batter.

Carefully remove onion rings from air fryer after each batch and serve.

spicy green beans with shallots, garlic, and ginger

Serves 6

These green beans are full of bold flavor and are great topped with toasted almonds and served very simply with steamed brown rice.

1 shallot, sliced thinly

1 clove garlic, minced

1 small jalapeño, seeded and minced

1 pound green beans

1 to 1 ½ tablespoons grated fresh ginger

3 tablespoons Bragg Liquid Aminos or soy sauce

kosher salt and coarsely ground black pepper, to taste

Heat a large skillet over medium high heat. Add the shallots and sauté for about 5 minutes, or until they begin to soften. Add a bit of water to avoid sticking to the pan, as needed. Once they start to brown, add garlic and jalapeño, and continue to cook for about 30 seconds.

Add the green beans to the hot pan, along with the ginger and Bragg Liquid Aminos. Turn down the heat to medium and stir frequently until the beans are well coated with the sauce and become just tender-crisp. Season with salt and pepper and serve immediately.

roasted butternut squash, onions, and beets

Serves 6 to 8

Butternut squash and beets are mood-lifting, low in fat, full of fiber, and fabulously heart-healthy, offering anti-inflammatory benefits that may reduce the risk of many chronic illnesses. Enjoy these roasted gems with mashed potatoes and steamed broccoli for a nourishing meal that's simple and delicious.

1 ½ pounds butternut squash, chopped into ¾-inch cubes

1 large onion, diced

2 small beets, peeled and chopped into ½-inch cubes

½ cup water (or more, if needed)

kosher salt and coarsely ground black pepper, to taste

dash of cayenne pepper or Cajun or Creole seasoning, to taste (optional)

garnish: fresh parsley or cilantro, minced (optional)

Preheat oven to 400 degrees.

Place vegetables in a nonstick roasting pan, with ¼ cup water. Add the seasoning and combine evenly.

Roast uncovered for 20 minutes, then stir gently, and add another splash of water (¼ cup or more) if needed. Continue to roast for another 25 to 35 minutes, or until very tender.

Remove from oven, garnish with fresh herbs if desired, and serve warm.

easy air-fried potatoes

Serves 2

This very simple potato recipe has limitless possibilities, and makes a terrific savory side dish, and equally delicious breakfast, lunch or afternoon snack.

---

1 or 2 leftover baked russet potatoes

kosher salt and coarsely ground
black pepper, to taste

Optional dipping sauce* (see below)

Slice potatoes in half length-wise, and each half into quarters, so that you have 8 wedges from each potato. Lightly sprinkle both sides with salt and pepper.

Place in air fryer basket and bake around 12 to 14 minutes at 375 degrees.

Once potatoes are golden and crispy, carefully remove from air fryer.

Serve with unsweetened ketchup, or dipping sauce.

* For an easy dipping sauce, mix together unsweetened nondairy yogurt, hot sauce, and green salsa.

steamed kale and cabbage

Makes approximately 4 cups

Here's my super simple method to make these very pretty greens. I use pre-washed lacinato kale (also called Tuscan or dinosaur kale) along with shredded cabbage slaw. Super easy, and good as gold, drizzled with balsamic vinegar.

10 ounces chopped (washed, ready to use) lacinato kale (also called Tuscan or dinosaur kale)

9 ounces shredded green and red cabbage slaw

1 ½ cups water

In a large electric pressure cooker, add kale and cabbage mixture. Add water. Lock the lid in place.

Select High Pressure and set the timer for 3 minutes. After cooking is complete, allow pot to rest for 2 to 3 minutes, and then use the quick release method to release the remainder of the pressure. When valve drops, carefully remove lid.

Serve piping hot with balsamic vinegar. Extra steamed greens can be refrigerated for use later in the week.

roasted carrots, potatoes, and onions

Serves 4

*Roasting root vegetables is a classic food preparation method,
and usually involves oil. I substitute water instead, and still
keep every drop of comforting flavor.*

1 ½ pounds red-skinned or Yukon Gold potatoes, chopped into ¾-inch cubes

1 ½ pounds carrots, chopped into ¾-inch pieces

1 large onion, diced into ¼-inch pieces

½ cup water (or more, if needed)

kosher salt and coarsely ground black pepper, to taste

Cajun or Creole seasoning, to taste

1 teaspoon dried dill (or more, to taste)

Preheat oven to 400 degrees.

Place vegetables in a nonstick roasting pan with ¼ cup water. Add the seasoning (except dill) and combine gently.

Roast uncovered for 40 minutes, then stir gently, and add another ¼ cup of water (or slightly more) if needed. Continue to roast for another 20 minutes, or until all of the vegetables are nice and tender. Remove from oven.

Finish with dill, and additional salt and pepper (if needed), and serve immediately.

chimichurri corn on the cob

Serves 6

Chimichurri Sauce has an amazing depth of flavor that enhances just about anything and everything savory and plant-based. With fresh parsley, cilantro, and basil, it's especially delicious brushed over corn on the cob.

CHIMICHURRI SAUCE

1 cup fresh flat-leaf parsley

1 cup fresh cilantro

1 cup fresh basil

3 tablespoons water

2 tablespoons apple cider vinegar

½ clove garlic

juice of ½ lime

¼ teaspoon kosher salt (or to taste)

⅛ teaspoon cayenne pepper

⅛ teaspoon coarsely ground black pepper

CORN ON THE COB

6 ears corn on the cob, husks and silk removed

Place the Chimichurri Sauce ingredients in a high-powered blender, and process until smooth. Set aside.

Using your favorite method, cook fresh corn until tender-crisp. I like steaming the corn in either a glass-covered steaming basket or in a large nonstick skillet with an inch or so of water.

Once corn is tender, remove from heat, slather hot corn with Chimichurri Sauce, and serve immediately.

Refrigerate remainder of the sauce for another time.

homemade baked beans

Serves 8 to 9

I grew up with canned baked beans, but now I make them myself, and they are so much better. This is fabulous served with Favorite Baked Tempeh Burgers, page 117 Chimichuri Corn on the Cob, page 149 and Creamy Cabbage and Apple Slaw, page 106.

1 onion, diced

3 14-ounce cans navy beans, rinsed and drained

1 8-ounce can tomato sauce (no sugar, no oil)

4 tablespoons date syrup

4 tablespoons unsweetened ketchup

4 teaspoons yellow mustard

1 teaspoon hot sauce

1 teaspoon kosher salt (or to taste)

½ teaspoon coarsely ground black pepper

Heat a large nonstick skillet over high heat. Add onions and dry sauté until translucent. Sprinkle a little bit of water as needed to prevent sticking to the pan. When soft and golden, remove from heat and set aside.

Meanwhile, mix all other ingredients in a medium saucepan. Bring to a simmer. Add sautéed onions. Combine well. Remove from heat.

Carefully pour the beans mixture into medium size (3- or 4-quart) slow cooker to finish cooking. Cover and cook on Low setting for 2 or 3 hours, or until sauce thickens a little bit, and the beans are tender and flavorful.

Serve hot and enjoy.

air-fried zucchini

Serves 2

Zucchini is one of my favorite vegetables in any savory dish, from scrambled tofu, to burritos... you name it. But air-fried, zucchini is good enough to eat all by itself.

---

2 medium zucchini

sprinkle of smoked salt (optional)

chile lime seasoning blend (optional)

Prepare zucchini into ½-inch cubes or quartered slices. Sprinkle very lightly with smoked salt, and chile lime seasoning blend (if desired).

Layer zucchini in the basket of your air fryer and bake at 400 degrees for around 15 minutes or until golden and tender in the center, tossing once or twice during cooking time to ensure even baking.

Carefully remove from air fryer and enjoy.

harissa-spiced butternut squash air fries

Serves 2 to 4

The hardest part of using butternut squash (no pun intended) is slicing it, right? I love a good shortcut, so I'm always happy to see it already prepped in the produce section. Use diced or chopped if you can't find crinkle-cut and look for a harissa seasoning blend in your spice aisle, made with paprika, red chili pepper, cayenne, coriander, and cumin. It's hot, spicy, and full of flavor.

12 ounces butternut squash, sliced like crinkle-cut French fries

1 teaspoon harissa seasoning

kosher salt, to taste

Toss the butternut squash crinkle cuts with harissa seasoning and salt.

Place in the basket of your air fryer and bake at 400 degrees for around 12 to 14 minutes, or until tender and crispy.

Carefully remove from air fryer and serve immediately.

pan-steamed broccolini with toasted pistachios

Serves 2 to 3

Only two ingredients (plus seasonings), but this combination is almost magical. Tender, crunchy, salty, slightly bitter, and just a tad smoky, it's super easy and really good.

---

1 bunch fresh broccolini, rinsed and trimmed

handful of raw pistachios

kosher salt and coarsely ground black pepper, to taste

pinch of smoked paprika (optional)

Heat a large nonstick skillet over high heat. Place broccolini into the hot pan along with a little sprinkle of water.

Toss the broccolini occasionally as it pan-steams, to ensure even distribution of the heat.

Once the broccolini begins to turn a bright green color and is almost fork tender, toss the pistachios into the pan to lightly toast along with the broccolini for an additional 30 seconds or so. Avoid overcooking.

Remove from heat, season to taste, and serve immediately.

baked potato, sweet potato, and zucchini latkes

Makes approximately 24 latkes

*Traditional potato latkes are skillet fried in a pool of oil, but these
are baked in a hot oven instead. Not a bit heavy or greasy, these are
100% regret-free and healthfully delicious.*

4 medium russet or Yukon Gold potatoes, scrubbed, unpeeled, and shredded

1 medium sweet potato, peeled and shredded

1 medium zucchini, shredded

1 medium Vidalia onion, minced

⅜ cup oat flour

2 tablespoons ground flaxseed meal

1 ½ tablespoons nutritional yeast

1 ½ teaspoons kosher salt (or to taste)

½ teaspoon coarsely ground black pepper

Preheat oven to 425 degrees. Have ready an oven-safe non-stick griddle, or a baking sheet lined with a silicone baking mat.

Place the shredded potatoes, shredded sweet potatoes, shredded zucchini, and minced onion in a large colander in the sink, and allow excess moisture to drain.

In a large bowl, mix together the flour, flax, nutritional yeast, salt, and pepper.

Squeeze out the excess liquid from the vegetables in the colander, one handful at a time. Add the vegetables to the large bowl of seasoned flour and combine well.

Scoop out rounded heaping tablespoons of the latke batter, and place on the baking sheets to create 3-inch pancakes. Use a spoon or spatula to flatten evenly. (Keeping these pancakes on the thin side will help them bake more evenly.)

Bake for about 20 minutes or until golden brown, flipping at around 15. Remove from oven and serve warm.

cremini mushroom sauce with shallots and madeira wine

Makes approximately 3 cups

I created this by request for one of my clients who asked if I'd make a light mushroom gravy for her to use over baked potatoes. It's wonderful for holidays served with Toasted Bread Stuffing With Potatoes, Sweet Potatoes, and Fresh Herbs too (page 163).

2 shallots, sliced

8 ounces cremini (or white button) mushrooms, cleaned, stems removed, and chopped

¾ cup Madeira wine

2 cups mushroom broth, divided

¼ cup raw cashews

1 teaspoon balsamic vinegar

1 ½ teaspoons Bragg Liquid Aminos or soy sauce

pinch of poultry seasoning

2 teaspoons cornstarch

¾ teaspoon kosher salt (or to taste)

¼ teaspoon coarsely ground black pepper (or to taste)

small handful of fresh Italian parsley or cilantro, minced

Heat a large skillet, and sauté shallots and mushrooms in the wine. Turn down the heat slightly, and continue cooking for a few minutes, until the shallots and mushrooms are soft and golden.

In a high-powered blender, add 1 cup (only) of mushroom broth, the cashews, balsamic vinegar, Bragg Liquid Aminos, and poultry seasoning, along with up to one-half of the shallot and mushroom mixture. Process together until very smooth and creamy.

Stir the blended cashew mixture into the mushrooms, shallots, and wine on the stove. Simmer over very low heat.

In a separate bowl, make a slurry, whisking together the cornstarch and remaining 1 cup of broth. Gradually whisk slurry mixture into the mushroom sauce on the stove, carefully stirring to prevent lumps. Allow the sauce to simmer gently, until liquid has reduced by almost one-third. Season with salt and pepper, and finish with fresh herbs. Stir well, remove from heat, and serve hot over potatoes, pasta, brown rice, or bread stuffing.

toasted bread stuffing with potatoes, sweet potatoes, and fresh herbs

Serves 8 to 10

This Toasted Bread Stuffing with Potatoes, Sweet Potatoes, and Fresh Herbs has just the right touch of cozy flavors and chewy goodness, and is absolutely perfect for Thanksgiving, the holiday season, and all winter long.

2 large onions, diced

2 large stalks celery, diced

4 slices sprouted whole grain bread

4 Yukon Gold potatoes, baked or microwaved, peeled, ½-inch cubes

1 sweet potato, baked or microwaved, peeled, ½-inch cubes

1 ¾ cups vegetable broth

kosher salt and coarsely ground black pepper, to taste

dash of Cajun or Creole seasoning

handful of fresh Italian parsley, minced

8 to 10 sprigs of fresh thyme, minced

4 to 5 leaves of rosemary, minced

Preheat oven to 375 degrees. Have ready a large ceramic baking dish.

Heat a large nonstick skillet over high heat. Add onions and celery and dry sauté until translucent. Sprinkle a little bit of water as needed to prevent sticking to the pan.

Meanwhile, toast bread slices. Cut slices of warm toast into ½-inch cubes, and add to a large bowl, along with cubed potatoes, sweet potatoes, and broth. Combine well, moistening all the bread.

Smash slightly to break up the potatoes a little further. Season well with salt, pepper, and a dash of Cajun or Creole seasoning. Mix in sautéed vegetables and fresh herbs. Pour mixture into a ceramic baking dish and bake for 40 minutes, or until the top is golden. Remove from oven and serve immediately.

fresh raw cranberry sauce

Serves 8

This is THE best cranberry sauce I have ever had. It isn't cooked, so it's a little crisp, a little sweet, and a little tart, and it's the absolute easiest too.

12 ounces fresh cranberries

2 apples, peeled, cored, and quartered

1 orange, peeled and quartered

⅔ cup dates, pits removed

Rinse and towel-dry the cranberries.

Place the cranberries along with all other ingredients in a food processor bowl, and pulse together briefly until desired texture is achieved (somewhat diced, somewhat chunky).

Serve immediately at room temperature or refrigerate to serve chilled.

mouth-watering mains

colcannon stuffed baked potatoes

Serves 4

Inspired by traditional Irish Colcannon, these potatoes are mashed, seasoned, combined with sautéed red cabbage and onions, and stuffed right back into the shells. A splash of balsamic vinegar adds extra color and flavor.

4 medium Russet potatoes

1 medium Vidalia onion, diced

4 cups shredded red cabbage (or shredded red cabbage slaw mix)

kosher salt and coarsely ground black pepper, to taste

3 tablespoons balsamic vinegar

½ cup plain, unsweetened nondairy milk (or just enough to mash potatoes)

dash of Cajun or Creole seasoning (or to taste)

garnish: fresh cilantro (optional)

Preheat oven to 375 degrees.

Prepare potatoes for baking by washing well and poking several times with a fork or knife for steam to escape during baking.

Bake for approximately one hour, or until fork tender. Remove from oven and allow to rest.

Meanwhile, sauté diced onions in a nonstick skillet over medium-high heat. Add just enough water to prevent sticking. Once onions begin to soften, add cabbage, and continue to sauté for a few minutes, until cabbage just begins to soften. Do not overcook. Mix in balsamic vinegar. Remove from heat and set aside.

Once potatoes are cool enough to touch, slice potatoes lengthwise. Scoop insides of potatoes into a bowl, being careful not to tear the skins. Leave a small rim of potato intact for support. Sprinkle potato skins with salt.

Mash the potato flesh in the bowl, along with enough milk to achieve the right mashed/smashed potato consistency. Season with salt and pepper, and a few dashes of Cajun or Creole seasoning, to taste.

Mix in cabbage and onions. Spoon potato mixture back into the potato shells evenly until each half is rounded and almost overflowing.

Warm briefly (in the oven, toaster oven, microwave or air fryer) for a few minutes, until heated all the way through.

Remove from oven, garnish with fresh cilantro (if desired), and serve immediately.

creamy tomato and fresh basil pasta sauce

Serves approximately 10

This sauce is a family favorite and I make it almost weekly. It's quick and easy, but so wonderful that I often serve this for company, too. Shallots deglazed in wine add tantalizing depth, and fresh basil adds just the right final touch. Extra sauce freezes perfectly.

1 large sweet onion, diced

1 shallot, diced

1 cup white or red wine

1 28-ounce can diced or crushed tomatoes

1 6-ounce can tomato paste

2 teaspoons kosher salt (or to taste)

½ teaspoon coarsely ground black pepper

¾ cup raw cashews

2 cups vegetable broth

1 cup fresh basil leaves, minced

Heat large pot over high heat. Add the onion, and steam sauté until the onion becomes translucent. Add the shallot to the hot pan and deglaze the pan with the wine. Continue to sauté the vegetables until golden and caramelized. Sprinkle a little bit of water as needed to prevent sticking to the pan.

Mix in the tomatoes and tomato paste. Season with salt and pepper. Bring mixture almost to a boil, combining thoroughly, then reduce to simmer, and allow to cook, covered, for about eight minutes. Use an immersion blender (if desired) to process the sauce to desired texture (slightly smooth, yet still a little chunky).

Meanwhile, place the cashews and the broth in a high-powered blender. Process for a minute or so, until very smooth. Stir the cashew cream into the pot of simmering tomato sauce. Combine well, and continue simmering together (covered), until the sauce has thickened slightly, for a few minutes more.

Stir in fresh basil and serve immediately over hot whole wheat pasta.

ginger baby bok choy stir fry with spicy tofu

Serves 4

Baby bok choy, a member of the cabbage family, is mild and sweet, and, once cooked, the stalks look a little like celery and the leaves resemble collards. This dish creates an irresistible fusion of flavors, with tangy fresh ginger and sweet bright citrus.

½ cup leeks, trimmed, rinsed, and sliced (or ⅓ cup sweet onion, diced)

1 large carrot, cut into very thin julienne strips

1 tablespoon grated fresh ginger

juice of 1 orange (approximately ½ cup)

2 tablespoons Bragg Liquid Aminos or soy sauce

1 tablespoon rice vinegar

1 ½ pounds baby bok choy or regular bok choy, trimmed, rinsed, and sliced thinly (using both the leaves and stalks)

Spicy Tofu (recipe below)

Heat a large wok or skillet with ¼ cup of water. Sauté leeks and carrots for about 5 minutes, or until soft and tender.

Stir in the ginger, orange juice, Bragg Liquid Aminos, and vinegar. Add the bok choy greens and leaves. Bring to a boil, reduce to simmer, and continue to cook until greens are wilted and bright green, about 2 to 4 minutes.

Add Spicy Tofu on top of the bok choy mixture, and gently stir for one minute to heat through. Serve immediately over steamed brown rice.

spicy tofu

1 package extra firm tofu, diced or crumbled

splash of Bragg Liquid Aminos or soy sauce

splash of hot sauce

Heat a large skillet or wok with ¼ cup of water. Add tofu to the pan and brown slightly, stirring occasionally. Sprinkle to taste with Bragg Liquid Aminos and hot sauce.

Continue to cook until browned well. Turn off heat and set aside.

hearty lentil shepherd's pie

Serves 12

This holiday-worthy dish makes everyone happy with a savory lentil stew simmered with onions and red wine, smothered by rich mashed potatoes, and baked in a hot oven until bubbling and golden brown.

¾ cup fresh bread crumbs (I like making them from Ezekiel bread)

6 large Yukon Gold potatoes, or 5 Yukon Gold and 1 large sweet potato

½ cup unsweetened soy milk

kosher salt and coarsely ground black pepper, to taste

1 large onion, minced

2 stalks celery, diced

1 medium zucchini, diced

3 ¼ cups cooked lentils or 2 (15-ounce) cans of lentils, rinsed and drained

3 tablespoons red wine

3 tablespoons vegetable broth

1 tablespoon Bragg Liquid Aminos or soy sauce

4 tablespoons tomato paste or prepared chili sauce

1 teaspoon cumin

dash of Creole or Cajun seasoning

kosher salt and coarsely ground black pepper, to taste

8 to 10 ounces baby spinach or arugula leaves, chopped

Preheat oven to 400 degrees. Have ready two deep-dish pie pans OR one 9-inch x 13-inch baking pan. Scatter the breadcrumbs evenly over the bottom of the pan(s) and set aside.

Peel and chop the potatoes. Place in a large saucepan with enough water to cover. Salt the water (if desired). Bring potatoes to boil, reduce heat to simmer, cover saucepan, and cook until tender. Drain and transfer potatoes to a large mixing bowl. Add soy milk, and salt and pepper to taste, and mash until fluffy, using more milk if needed. Set aside.

While the potatoes are cooking, heat a large nonstick skillet. Add onion and celery and sauté over medium heat until translucent, adding water as needed to prevent sticking. Add zucchini and lentils and bring to a gentle simmer.

Stir in wine, broth, Bragg Liquid Aminos, tomato paste or chili sauce, and seasonings. Cook gently for a few minutes, until zucchini is tender.

Add spinach or arugula to skillet, stirring in a little at a time, just until wilted. Remove from heat, taste, and adjust seasonings to your liking.

Pour the lentil mixture into prepared pan(s). Spread the mashed potatoes evenly over the top. If using two pie plates, divide mixtures evenly between them.

Bake uncovered for 35 minutes, or until bubbling hot, and potatoes begin to turn golden brown and slightly crispy. Remove from oven and allow to stand for five minutes. Serve hot.

mac and cheese perfection

Serves 8

This cheesy vegan pasta… well… I think it's so heavenly that I had to name it accordingly. The cream sauce is magical, made with a blended mixture of cashews, roasted red peppers, and grilled onions. It's addictively comforting and delicious.

16 ounces whole wheat or brown rice pasta

1 onion, diced

1 cup raw cashews

1 cup unsweetened nondairy milk

½ cup water

1 6-ounce jar of roasted red peppers, rinsed

¼ cup nutritional yeast

2 tablespoons fresh lemon juice

2 tablespoons vegetable broth

2 teaspoons yellow mustard

2 ½ teaspoons salt (or to taste)

dash of cayenne pepper (optional)

Preheat oven to 400 degrees.

Heat a large nonstick skillet over high heat. Add onions and dry sauté until translucent. Sprinkle a little bit of water as needed to prevent sticking to the pan.

Meanwhile, cook pasta according to package directions. Drain and set aside.

In a high-powered blender, combine the cooked onion with cashews, milk, water, roasted red peppers, nutritional yeast, lemon juice, broth, mustard, salt, and cayenne, and blend until smooth.

Pour mixture into a large baking dish. Add cooked pasta and combine well.

Bake uncovered 15 to 20 minutes, or until golden. Serve immediately.

indonesian peanut sauté

Serves approximately 6

This peanut sauce with fresh basil and lime juice is served over noodles and tender-crisp red cabbage and onions. It's a winning combination with just the right flavor and crunch.

½ pound whole wheat angel hair pasta

¼ cup vegetable broth

¼ cup water (or more if needed)

1 onion, sliced

1 large carrot, cut into thin strips

1 clove garlic, minced

2 cups red cabbage, thinly sliced

2 cups broccoli florets

¼ cup fresh basil, chopped

¼ cup natural peanut butter

¼ cup Bragg Liquid Aminos or soy sauce

2 tablespoons rice vinegar

1 tablespoon grated fresh ginger

2 tablespoons date syrup

1 teaspoon hot sauce

kosher salt, to taste

juice of 1 fresh lime

Prepare pasta. Drain and set aside.

Heat a large nonstick pan over high medium-heat. Add broth, water, onions and carrot. Sauté for 5 minutes, or until vegetables are slightly cooked. Add the garlic, cabbage, and broccoli, and continue to cook for a couple of minutes until the broccoli turns bright green but is still tender-crisp. Stir in cooked pasta and fresh basil. Set aside.

In a separate saucepan, mix peanut butter, Bragg Liquid Aminos, rice vinegar, ginger, date syrup, and hot sauce. Cook over medium heat, stirring until mixture is smooth. Pour over noodle mixture. Season with a touch of salt.

Squeeze lime juice over the dish and serve immediately.

spicy black beans and greens over rice

Serves 4

I originally created this recipe upon request for the T. Colin Campbell Center for Nutrition Studies Plant-Based Food Guide: How to Eat Well on a Budget, and it checks all the boxes: extra easy, wallet-friendly, and nutrition-packed.

---

2 cups prepared black beans, or 1 (15-ounce) can, rinsed and drained

¾ cup fresh salsa (or to taste)

4 cups raw greens, stems stripped, and leaves rinsed and chopped

kosher salt and coarsely ground black pepper, to taste

4 cups cooked brown rice (warm)

garnishes: avocado, chopped tomatoes, diced bell peppers, and fresh cilantro or basil

Heat black beans in a large saucepan. Stir in salsa and chopped greens. Cover, and steam until the greens are tender. Season with salt and pepper.

Serve over warm brown rice, along with toasted corn tortillas. Top with your choice of avocado, chopped tomatoes, diced bell peppers, and fresh cilantro or basil.

creamy vegetable lasagna

Serves 8

I like to prepare a few steps of this dreamy wonder earlier in the day so that when it's time to build the layers, everything comes together quickly. That way, all that's left to do is slide the pan into a hot oven, set the table, and relax.

SAUCE

1 quart of homemade pasta sauce (Creamy Tomato and Fresh Basil Pasta Sauce, page 171, OR Cozy Lentil Bolognese, page 191), OR 1 jar of your favorite no-oil-added tomato-based pasta sauce

PASTA

8 to 12 ounces whole wheat lasagna noodles

CREAMY CASHEW CHEESE SAUCE WITH FRESH BASIL

¼ cup raw cashews

1 cup hot water

2 tablespoons tapioca flour

1 tablespoon nutritional yeast

1 teaspoon fresh lemon juice

½ teaspoon salt (or to taste)

⅛ teaspoon coarsely ground black pepper

¼ cup fresh basil leaves (loosely packed), minced

CREAMED GREENS

2 shallots or 1 medium onion, sliced

1 cup vegetable broth (more if needed)

¼ cup white wine

8 cups fresh dark leafy greens, chopped (I like a mixture of baby kale, baby spinach, and arugula)

1 tablespoon nutritional yeast

pinch of nutmeg

⅓ cup raw cashews

⅓ cup water

kosher salt and coarsely ground black pepper, to taste

Have handy one quart of red pasta sauce and set aside.

Cook the lasagna noodles and set aside.

To prepare Creamed Greens, place the shallots in a hot skillet. Dry-sauté over medium heat for a few minutes, stirring frequently. Once they begin to caramelize, add the vegetable broth and wine, and simmer until the shallots are tender. Then add the greens, combine well, and cook just until wilted.

Add nutritional yeast and nutmeg.

Meanwhile, in a high-powered blender, blend

⅓ cup cashews with ⅓ cup water, until very smooth and creamy. Mix the cashew cream into the pan of hot greens and continue to cook until the sauce has thickened slightly. Remove from heat. Season with salt and pepper and set aside.

To prepare Creamy Cashew Cheese Sauce with Fresh Basil, place ¼ cup cashews, 1 cup hot water, tapioca flour, nutritional yeast, lemon juice, salt, and pepper in high-powered blender, and process until very smooth. Pour the mixture into a small skillet or saucepan and bring the heat to medium high. Stir continuously for a few minutes, until the sauce begins to look like a topping of thick melted cheese. Remove from heat, stir in minced fresh basil, and set aside.

Preheat oven to 375 degrees.

Into a 9-inch x 13-inch baking dish, layer 1 cup of sauce, and spread evenly on bottom of the pan. Add a layer of cooked noodles (about a third of the full amount), then another cup of sauce. Spread evenly. Add ½ of the creamed greens and spread evenly.

Add another layer of cooked noodles (half of the remainder), then another cup of sauce, and the rest of the greens.

Layer on the remainder of the noodles, and then the rest of the tomato sauce. Finish with the Creamy Cashew Cheese Sauce with Fresh Basil.

Cover the baking pan with foil and bake lasagna for 25 minutes. Carefully uncover the pan, and bake for an additional 20 to 25 minutes, or until the top begins to turn golden brown.

Remove from the oven and allow to rest for 5 to 10 minutes before serving.

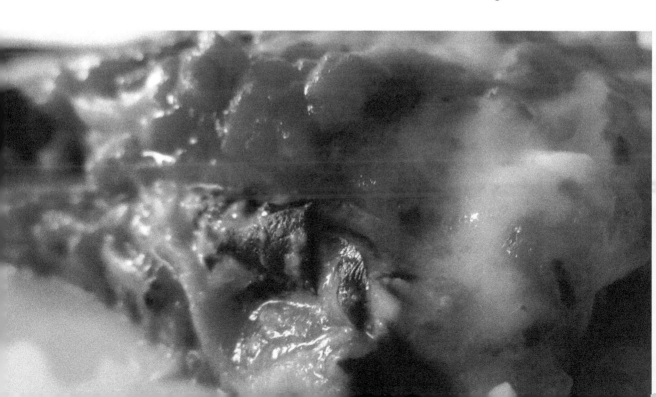

mashed potato stacks with mixed greens

Serves 2 to 3

Mashed potatoes with mixed greens are meant for each other, and these simple ingredients are somehow far from ordinary once combined. I love a mixture of chopped kale, Brussels sprouts, broccoli, green cabbage, and/or red cabbage, but any greens you like best will be delicious.

1 to 1 ½ cups steamed greens and/or steamed green vegetables, seasoned well*

3 to 4 cups mashed potatoes (see below)

Alternately layer hot greens with warm mashed potatoes, starting and ending with greens, into several individual small ramekins or bowls. Smooth over and carefully press each of the layers onto the one below, to flatten as much as possible before adding the next layer.

Once the layers are complete, carefully release the edges with a small offset spatula. Unmold from ramekins (or bowls) onto plates and serve.

* Season cooked greens with salt and pepper and fresh herbs, or with a light dressing of lemon juice, or yellow mustard and balsamic vinegar.

mashed potatoes

4 to 6 Yukon Gold potatoes

unsweetened soy milk

sprinkle of onion powder

coarsely ground black pepper and kosher salt, to taste

To make mashed potatoes, peel, and chop potatoes. Place potatoes in a pot of water and bring to a boil. Cover, reduce heat, and continue to simmer until tender.

Drain potatoes, and mash until creamy with soy milk and seasonings, to taste.

pasta with spinach and smoky red pepper romesco sauce

Serves 8

Try this no-cook sauce for a pasta dish that's rich, smoky, and unforgettably delicious. It's so quick, you won't believe it. Perfect to serve holiday guests, yet easy enough for any night of the week.

¾ cup toasted almonds

¼ cup fresh parsley or cilantro

1 15-ounce can tomato sauce (no sugar, no oil)

1 12-ounce jar of roasted red peppers, rinsed

2 tablespoons fresh lemon juice

2 tablespoons balsamic vinegar

1 teaspoon smoked paprika

1 teaspoon kosher salt (or to taste)

½ teaspoon cayenne pepper

16 ounces whole wheat pasta

16 ounces fresh baby spinach, roughly chopped

Into a high-powered blender, add almonds, parsley or cilantro, tomato sauce, roasted red peppers, lemon juice, balsamic vinegar, smoked paprika, salt, and cayenne pepper.

Blend until very smooth.

Meanwhile, cook pasta according to package directions. Before draining, stir in the spinach and allow the spinach to wilt in the hot water. Drain well and toss hot spinach and pasta mixture with the sauce.

Serve immediately.

stuffed baked potatoes

Serves 2

One of my favorite ways to enjoy baked potatoes is scooped out, mashed, and stuffed right back into the shells. The skins are crunchy on the outside, and the filling is pure creamy goodness on the inside. These are so simple yet satisfying beyond expectation.

2 large Russet or Yukon Gold potatoes, about 8 ounces each

⅓ cup unsweetened nondairy milk

1 cup cooked vegetables finely chopped (onions, broccoli, cauliflower, etc.)

4 tablespoons oil-free hummus

½ teaspoon hot sauce

½ teaspoon kosher salt (or to taste)

Preheat oven to 375 degrees. Prepare potatoes for baking by washing well and poking several times with a fork or knife for steam to escape during baking.

Bake for approximately one hour, or until fork tender. Remove from oven and allow to rest until cool enough to touch. Slice potatoes lengthwise.

Scoop insides of potatoes into a bowl, being careful not to tear the skins. Leave a small rim of potato intact for support.

Lay the hollowed-out potato shells onto a baking sheet.

Mash the potato flesh in a bowl along with the remaining ingredients, combining thoroughly. Spoon mixture back into the potato shells, filling evenly until each half is rounded and almost overflowing. Pop them back into the oven, and bake until heated all the way through, approximately 15 minutes.

Remove from oven and serve immediately.

cozy lentil bolognese

Makes approximately 1 quart of sauce

Sautéed vegetables, hearty lentils, and a kick from jalapeño elevate this sauce into a rich, company-worthy meal, perfect for family and friends of every dietary persuasion.

1 onion, diced

1 or 2 clove(s) garlic, minced

1 red, yellow, or orange bell pepper, diced

1 zucchini, diced

1 yellow summer squash, diced

1 jalapeño pepper, minced

3 cups cooked brown lentils

1 28-ounce can tomato sauce (no sugar, no oil)

¾ to 1 cup white wine

2 teaspoons salt (or to taste)

½ teaspoon coarsely ground black pepper

sprinkle of Cajun or Creole seasoning (optional)

splash of balsamic vinegar

garnish: fresh basil

Heat a medium size nonstick stock pot over medium-high heat. Add the onion, and dry-sauté until the onion becomes translucent. Sprinkle a little bit of water as needed to prevent sticking to the pan.

Once the onion is tender, add the garlic, bell pepper, zucchini, summer squash, and jalapeño, and continue to cook for a few minutes more until the vegetables are just tender. Add lentils, tomato sauce, and wine. Bring mixture to a boil, stirring thoroughly. Immediately cover the pot, reduce heat, and continue to simmer, covered, for a few more minutes, just until sauce is slightly thickened. Season with salt and pepper, and (if desired) Cajun or Creole seasoning. Add splash of balsamic vinegar and mix well.

Garnish with fresh basil and serve immediately over hot pasta.

creamy avocado sauce with fresh basil and lime

Serves 4

This sauce is a no-cook wonder. It's perfect for a warm summer evening, and lovely topped with steamed broccoli, fresh tomatoes, or toasted pine nuts, or served with fresh corn on the cob.

1 ripe avocado

½ cup fresh basil leaves

6 tablespoons water

juice of 1 lime

½ teaspoon kosher salt (or to taste)

¼ teaspoon coarsely ground black pepper

2 or 3 splashes of hot sauce

8 ounces whole wheat angel hair pasta, uncooked

Place the flesh of the avocado in a food processor or high-powered blender. Add fresh basil leaves, water, lime juice, salt, pepper, and hot sauce. Blend until mixture is completely smooth and set aside.

Meanwhile, cook pasta in a large pot of boiling salted water until al dente. Drain noodles.

Serve sauce immediately over hot pasta.

three bean sweet potatoes and brussels sprouts

Serves 4

This very simple sweet potato entrée can help you get on track and stay on track with all of your plant-based goals. Make extras to have handy all week long — these are fiber-rich, full of flavor, and completely delicious.

4 sweet potatoes

1 10-ounce package shaved (or shredded) raw Brussels sprouts

1 15-ounce can Tri-Bean Blend (kidney, pinto, and black beans), rinsed and drained

1 tablespoon homemade Mexican seasoning (see right)

¼ cup water

kosher salt and coarsely ground black pepper, to taste

garnish: fresh cilantro (if desired)

Preheat the oven to 375 degrees.

Prepare sweet potatoes for baking by scrubbing, then poking several times with a fork or knife for steam to escape while baking. Place sweet potatoes on a parchment paper-lined baking sheet or in a nonstick roasting pan and roast for 45 or 50 minutes, or until nice and tender. Remove from oven.

While potatoes are baking, steam sauté Brussels sprouts in a large nonstick skillet over hot heat until almost tender, adding just enough water to avoid sticking. Set aside.

Meanwhile, in a small saucepan, combine beans with 1 tablespoon of Mexican seasoning along with ¼ cup of water. Bring to a boil; then quickly reduce to a simmer. Allow to heat through completely for a minute or two, until mixture is hot, bubbling, and slightly thickened.

While sweet potatoes are still warm from the oven, split in half lengthwise. Mash (just slightly) with a fork and season with salt and pepper. Top each sweet potato with Brussels sprouts and seasoned bean mixture.

Garnish (if desired) with fresh cilantro. Serve immediately.

homemade mexican seasoning

1 tablespoon chili powder

1 1/2 teaspoons cumin

1 teaspoon kosher salt (or to taste)

1/2 teaspoon coarsely ground black pepper

1/2 teaspoon paprika

1/4 teaspoon garlic powder

1/4 teaspoon onion powder

1/4 teaspoon oregano

1/8 teaspoon cayenne pepper

Mix ingredients together in a medium size bowl, and store in a small jar or airtight container.

* I make this seasoning ahead and store it in a little jar with my spices. I often multiply this recipe 4 times, which makes around one cup.

spicy black-eyed peas and baby kale

Serves 6 to 8

These budget-friendly beans and greens are served over creamy mashed potatoes, and they're so good, you may want it for breakfast, lunch, and dinner, and I'm only partly kidding.

1 large sweet onion, diced

1 large shallot, diced

2 or 3 stalks celery, diced

1 15-ounce can diced tomatoes

1 cup vegetable broth

2 cups pre-cooked black-eyed peas (or 15-ounce can, rinsed and drained)

¾ teaspoon cumin

½ teaspoon turmeric

½ teaspoon coriander

⅛ to ¼ teaspoon cayenne pepper (use more or less to taste)

1 ½ teaspoons kosher salt (or to taste)

½ teaspoon coarsely ground black pepper

4 cups raw baby kale, chopped

Heat a large pot over high heat. Add the onion, and dry sauté until the onion becomes translucent. Sprinkle a little bit of water as needed to prevent sticking to the pan. Add shallot and celery, and continue to sauté vegetables until golden.

To the sautéed vegetables, add tomatoes, broth, cooked black-eyed peas, and seasonings. Combine well. Toss the kale on top.

Bring mixture to a boil, then cover and reduce heat. Simmer together for 20 to 30 minutes, or until vegetables are all very tender. Remove lid and continue to simmer for a few minutes more, to reduce some of the liquid (if desired).

Serve beans and greens hot over creamy mashed potatoes, or alongside warmed sprouted whole grain tortillas.

brown rice bowl with smoky roasted red pepper cashew cream

Serves 8

This special rice bowl is topped with a truly spectacular sauce that's rich and indulgent with stunning color and jaw-dropping flavor.

1 red bell pepper, very roughly chopped, seeds removed *

1 cup raw cashews

½ cup water

1 tablespoon fresh lemon juice

1 tablespoon apple cider vinegar

1 teaspoon kosher salt (or to taste)

¾ teaspoon smoked paprika

¼ teaspoon yellow mustard

pinch of garlic powder

pinch of cayenne pepper

garnish: slices of fresh cucumber and carrots

Roast the red pepper* on a baking sheet in a 350 degree oven for about 30 minutes or until the skins are wrinkled and the pepper pieces are charred. Remove from oven and allow to rest just until cool enough to touch. Discard the charred skin if you wish. I leave the skin on.

Add the roasted red pepper to a high-powered blender with the cashews, water, lemon juice, vinegar, salt, smoked paprika, yellow mustard, garlic powder, and cayenne. Blend until smooth and creamy. Taste and adjust seasonings if needed.

Warm sauce briefly (if desired) and drizzle over bowls of steamed brown rice. Top bowls with sliced cucumbers and carrots and serve.

Instead of roasting a fresh bell pepper, you can substitute half of a 12-ounce jar of roasted red peppers (packed in water, not oil), drained, rinsed, and drained again.

warming soups and stews

sweet potato and cauliflower peanut stew

Serves 6 to 8

Simmering away on the stove, this comforting stew is the perfect antidote to a day that's cold and grey. With aromatic spices, fresh lemon, and peanut butter, this is soul-soothing goodness, and the culinary equivalent of a warm hug.

1 onion, chopped

1 clove garlic, minced

2 stalks celery, chopped

1 jalapeño, diced

2 sweet potatoes, peeled, diced into ½-inch cubes

1 cauliflower head, rinsed, chopped into 1-inch pieces

1 15-ounce can fire-roasted diced tomatoes

1 15-ounce can white beans, rinsed and drained

4 cups vegetable broth

2 cups water

1 ½ teaspoons chili powder

1 teaspoon coriander

1 teaspoon Berbere seasoning

½ teaspoon cumin

¼ teaspoon cayenne pepper

3 ½ teaspoons kosher salt (or to taste)

½ teaspoon coarsely ground black pepper

⅓ cup natural peanut butter

2 to 4 cups fresh baby spinach, roughly chopped

juice of 1 lemon

Heat a large soup pot. Add onion, and dry sauté until translucent, adding a little water as needed to prevent sticking to the pan. Add garlic, celery, and jalapeño and continue to sauté for another minute or two, stirring well.

Add the next 13 ingredients (sweet potatoes through black pepper). Bring to a boil, then cover and reduce to a rolling simmer for about 22 to 25 minutes, or until vegetables are tender.

Carefully add about 3 or 4 cups of the hot soup to a high-powered blender along with the peanut butter, and blend until smooth and creamy.

Return peanut mixture to soup pot. Combine well. Stir in spinach and lemon juice and allow spinach to wilt from the heat. Serve hot.

Serving suggestion – wonderful served over steamed whole wheat couscous, quinoa, or brown rice.

perfect lentil soup with mashed potatoes

Serves 8 to 10

This soup takes comfort food to a whole new level. I top it with warm mashed potatoes, using my usual oil-free method… just boil potatoes until tender, add unsweetened soy milk, salt and pepper, and smash until deliciously creamy.

1 large Vidalia onion, chopped

4 stalks celery, chopped

2 cups uncooked brown or green lentils, sorted and rinsed

9 cups vegetable broth

1 15-ounce can chopped or crushed tomatoes

1 teaspoon cumin

1/2 teaspoon curry powder

1/2 teaspoon garam masala

2 teaspoons kosher salt (or to taste)

1/2 teaspoon coarsely ground black pepper

1 bay leaf

1/4 cup fresh lemon juice

garnish: scoops of warm mashed potatoes

STOVETOP

Combine all ingredients in a large soup pot, except the lemon juice and mashed potatoes.

Bring to boil. Once boiling, reduce heat to simmer. Cover, and cook for one hour and 45 minutes, or until lentils are tender and begin to cook down to a smooth creamy soup.

Carefully remove the bay leaf. Use an immersion blender to create a slightly creamier texture (if desired). Stir in lemon juice. Serve hot, with scoops of mashed potatoes.

SLOW COOKER

Combine all ingredients in a large slow cooker, except the lemon juice and mashed potatoes.

Cover and cook on High setting for 6 hours or until lentils are tender. (All slow cookers have their own personality – older ones may take longer. Newer ones may take less time.)

Carefully remove the bay leaf. Use an immersion blender to create a slightly creamier texture (if desired). Stir in lemon juice. Serve hot, with scoops of mashed potatoes.

best veggie chili

Serves 10 to 12

One of my favorite comfort foods during our long winter months is this three-bean chili, layered with deep, satisfying flavors. Great served with warmed sprouted whole grain tortillas, or piled high over baked potatoes and garnished with fresh cilantro.

---

1 large onion, diced

3 stalks celery, chopped

2 carrots, diced

1 red bell pepper, chopped

1 teaspoon garlic, minced

1 15-ounce can black beans, rinsed and drained

1 15-ounce can red kidney beans, rinsed and drained

1 15-ounce can navy or pinto beans, rinsed and drained

1 15-ounce can diced tomatoes

1 15-ounce can diced tomatoes with jalapeños

1 6-ounce can tomato paste

2 to 3 cups vegetable broth (2 for slow cooker / 2 1/2 for electric pressure cooker / 3 for stovetop)

1/4 cup raisins, roughly chopped

1 1/2 tablespoons chili powder

2 teaspoons coriander

2 teaspoons cumin

1 to 2 tablespoons date syrup or molasses

1 tablespoon Dijon or brown mustard

1 tablespoon balsamic vinegar

2 1/2 teaspoons kosher salt (or to taste)

1/2 teaspoon coarsely ground black pepper

2 bay leaves

PRESSURE COOKER

In a large electric pressure cooker, add all ingredients to the cooking pot. Lock the lid in place. Select High Pressure and set the timer for 15 minutes.

Once the pressure cooking is complete, use the natural release method to release pressure for around 20 minutes, then quick release remainder of pressure. When valve drops, carefully remove lid.

Remove bay leaves. Taste and add additional seasoning (if desired). Serve with any combination of fresh cilantro, diced avocados, corn, baked potatoes, or warm tortillas.

SLOW COOKER

Add all ingredients to a large slow cooker. Mix well. Cover and cook on High setting for 5 or 6 hours, or Low for 8 to 10 hours.

Remove bay leaves. Taste and add additional seasoning (if desired). Serve with any combination of fresh cilantro, diced avocados, corn, baked potatoes, or warm tortillas.

STOVETOP

Add onion, celery, carrots, and bell pepper to a large soup pot. On medium-high heat, sauté in a small amount of water until almost tender. Add the garlic, and sauté for 1 minute more.

Add beans, tomato products, broth, and raisins. Mix well and add seasonings (chili powder through bay leaves). Bring to a boil. Reduce heat to rolling simmer, cover and cook for 90 minutes.

Remove bay leaves. Taste and add additional seasoning (if desired). Serve with any combination of fresh cilantro, diced avocados, corn, baked potatoes, or warm tortillas.

creamy cauliflower and carrot soup

Serves 8 to 10

This soup transforms ordinary vegetables into an entirely unexpected, velvety comfort food. Perfect served over steamed brown rice or with warm toasty sprouted whole grain bread, it's brimming with flavor, and loaded with fiber, vitamins and minerals.

4 cups baby carrots, divided

6 cups water, divided

1 onion, chopped

3 stalks celery, chopped

1 cauliflower head, washed, cut into 1-inch pieces

1 clove garlic, minced

4 teaspoons kosher salt (or to taste)

1 teaspoon coarsely ground black pepper

dash of cayenne pepper

dash of Creole or Cajun seasoning

½ teaspoon nutmeg

1 cup raw cashews

6 cups fresh baby spinach, roughly chopped

STOVETOP

In a high-powered blender add 2 cups of baby carrots with 2 cups of water. Blend until smooth. Set aside.

Thinly slice the other 2 cups of carrots.

To a large soup pot add the remaining 4 cups of water, blended carrot mixture, and the sliced carrots, plus the next 9 ingredients (onion through nutmeg).

Bring to a boil. Cover and reduce to a rolling simmer for 20 minutes, or until vegetables are tender. Remove soup from heat.

Using a ladle, place about 3 to 4 cups of the hot soup into a high-powered blender along with the raw cashews. Blend until smooth and creamy. Add cashew cream mixture back to soup pot and combine well.

Add the spinach and allow spinach to wilt from the heat. Serve hot.

PRESSURE COOKER

In a high-powered blender add 2 cups of baby carrots with 2 cups of water. Blend until smooth. Set aside.

Thinly slice the other 2 cups of carrots.

To a large electric pressure cooker add the remaining 4 cups of water, blended carrot mixture, and the sliced carrots, plus the next 9 ingredients (onion through nutmeg).

Lock the lid in place. Select High Pressure and set the timer for 12 minutes. After cooking is complete, use the quick release method to release the remainder of the pressure. When valve drops, carefully remove lid.

Using a ladle, place about 3 to 4 cups of the hot soup into a high-powered blender along with the raw cashews. Blend until smooth and creamy. Add cashew cream mixture back to soup pot and combine well.

Add the spinach and allow spinach to wilt from the heat. Serve hot.

red lentil soup

Serves 10 to 12

I have prepared this soup more times than I can count for large groups. It works its magic in just about an hour, and in all of its comforting glory is among my most requested recipes.

1 large Vidalia onion, chopped

3 or 4 stalks celery, chopped

8 cups vegetable broth

1 pound red lentils, sorted and rinsed

1 tablespoon cumin

1 ½ teaspoons coriander

1 teaspoon curry powder

¾ teaspoon turmeric

2 ½ teaspoons kosher salt (or to taste)

1 teaspoon coarsely ground black pepper

2 to 2 ¼ cups water

¼ cup fresh lemon juice

STOVETOP

Add all ingredients to a large soup pot, except the lemon juice. Bring to boil. Once boiling, reduce heat to a simmer. Cover, and cook for 1 hour and 15 minutes, stirring occasionally, until lentils cook down to a smooth creamy soup.

Use an immersion blender to create an even creamier texture (if desired).

Stir in lemon juice and serve hot.

PRESSURE COOKER

Add all ingredients to an electric pressure cooker, except the lemon juice.

Lock the lid in place. Select High Pressure and set the timer for 20 minutes. After cooking is complete, allow the pot to rest for about 10 minutes, and then use the quick release method to release the remainder of the pressure. When valve drops, carefully remove lid.

Use an immersion blender to create an even creamier texture (if desired).

Stir in lemon juice and serve hot.

Serving suggestion – wonderful with diced boiled potatoes, baby green peas, whole wheat pasta, or brown rice.

unstuffed cabbage

Serves 6 to 8

This is my daughter's favorite, and I love making this because it's deeply satisfying and extra delicious — without all the work of traditional stuffed cabbage.

---

1 large onion, diced

1 clove garlic, minced

1 large carrot, scrubbed or peeled

4 Medjool dates, pits removed

1 small head cabbage, cored and chopped into 1-inch cubes (around 9 cups)

1 cup vegetable broth

1 15-ounce can tomato sauce (no sugar, no oil)

½ teaspoon Hungarian paprika

½ teaspoon Berbere seasoning

2 teaspoons kosher salt (or to taste)

½ teaspoon coarsely ground black pepper

4 cups cooked brown rice

garnish: fresh chopped Italian parsley or cilantro

In a large electric pressure cooker, sauté the onion for a few minutes, using a little water to avoid sticking. Add garlic and stir for a minute (or less), and then select Cancel to stop the sauté process.

Meanwhile, in the bowl of a food processor, mince the carrot along with the dates, and set aside.

To the pressure-cooking pot, add the cabbage, vegetable broth, and tomato sauce. Stir in minced carrots and dates. Sprinkle in Hungarian paprika, Berbere seasoning, salt, and black pepper.

Lock the lid in place. Select High Pressure and set the timer for 8 minutes. After cooking is complete, allow the pot to rest for about 4 minutes, and then use the quick release method to release the remainder of the pressure. When valve drops, carefully remove lid. Add cooked brown rice and combine well until heated through.

Garnish with fresh chopped Italian parsley or cilantro and serve immediately.

red lentil and black bean soup

Serves 6 to 8

A squeeze of fresh orange juice brightens up a delicate balance of aromatic spices, simple red lentils and black beans, and the result is a bowl of nourishing bliss.

1 Vidalia onion, chopped

5 carrots, diced

5 stalks celery, diced

1 clove garlic, minced

1 ½ cups dried red lentils, sorted and rinsed

1 15-ounce can black beans, rinsed and drained

1 15-ounce can diced tomatoes

5 cups vegetable broth

2 teaspoons kosher salt (or to taste)

1 teaspoon coarsely ground black pepper

1 teaspoon cumin

1 teaspoon coriander

1 teaspoon turmeric

½ teaspoon chili powder

pinch of cayenne pepper

1 bay leaf

juice of 1 orange

STOVETOP

Combine all ingredients, except the juice of the orange, in a large soup pot.

Bring to boil. Once boiling, reduce heat to simmer. Cover, and cook for an hour and 15 minutes, or until lentils are creamy and soft, stirring occasionally.

Once lentils are tender, remove bay leaf. Stir in the juice of 1 orange.

Use an immersion blender to create a slightly creamier texture (if desired). Serve hot, with toasted sprouted whole grain bread.

PRESSURE COOKER

Combine all ingredients, except the juice of the orange, in an electric pressure cooker.

Lock the lid in place. Select High Pressure and set the timer for 20 minutes.

After cooking is complete, allow the pot to rest for about 10 minutes, and then use the quick release method to release the remainder of the pressure. When valve drops, carefully remove lid. Remove bay leaf. Stir in the juice of 1 orange.

Use an immersion blender to create a slightly creamier texture (if desired). Serve hot, with toasted sprouted whole grain bread.

creamy butternut squash soup with sweet corn and white beans

Serves 8 to 10

This is an easy recipe full of flavorful goodness. It makes a lasting impression with guests and leaves even non-vegans asking for more.

3 ½ to 4 cups vegetable broth (3 ½ for electric pressure cooker / 4 for stovetop)

1 large, sweet onion, diced

2 cloves garlic, minced

6 cups (approximately 2 pounds) butternut squash, peeled and cubed (fresh or frozen both work well)

1 10-ounce package frozen organic sweet corn

1 15-ounce can navy beans, rinsed and drained

½ teaspoon Cajun or Creole seasoning (or other seasoning of choice)

1 teaspoon kosher salt (or to taste)

½ teaspoon coarsely ground black pepper

garnish: fresh basil or cilantro

STOVETOP

In a large soup pot over medium-high heat, sauté onions in about ¼ cup of broth, for about five minutes, or until soft and translucent. Add garlic and continue to sauté for 30 seconds. Add squash, corn, beans, and the remainder of the broth.

Bring to a boil. Once boiling, reduce heat to simmer. Cover, and cook for about 20 minutes, or until the squash is tender, stirring occasionally. Add seasonings and mix thoroughly.

Using an immersion blender, create a mostly (but not entirely) creamy soup, leaving some pieces for texture. Taste and add additional seasoning (if desired) and garnish with fresh basil or cilantro.

PRESSURE COOKER

Combine all ingredients (except the garnish) in an electric pressure cooker.

Lock the lid in place. Select High Pressure and set timer for 10 minutes. After cooking is complete, use the quick release method to release pressure. When valve drops, carefully remove lid.

Using an immersion blender, create a mostly (but not entirely) creamy soup, leaving some pieces for texture. Taste and add additional seasoning (if desired) and garnish with fresh basil or cilantro.

lasagna minestrone

Serves 8 to 10

This one pot dish is a comforting cross between Minestrone Soup and a hearty pan of Lasagna, with vegetables, white beans, lasagna noodles, and greens cooked together in a tomato-rich broth.

1 large onion, diced

1 clove garlic, minced

2 to 3 cups chopped fresh vegetables (I like celery, red peppers, and zucchini)

4 cups vegetable broth

2 ½ cups water

1 15-ounce can crushed tomatoes

1 15-ounce can diced tomatoes

1 8-ounce can tomato sauce (no sugar, no oil)

⅓ cup tomato paste

6 to 10 ounces uncooked whole wheat lasagna noodles, broken into small pieces (see note to right)*

2 teaspoons kosher salt (or to taste)

½ teaspoon coarsely ground black pepper, or to taste

¼ teaspoon onion powder

⅓ cup raw cashews

1 15-ounce can navy beans, rinsed and drained

2 tablespoons nutritional yeast

¼ teaspoon red pepper flakes

2 cups fresh baby spinach, arugula or baby kale, roughly chopped

garnish: ½ cup fresh basil leaves, chopped

PRESSURE COOKER

Combine first 13 ingredients (onion through onion powder) in a large electric pressure cooker.

Lock the lid in place. Select High Pressure and set the timer for 4 minutes.

After cooking is complete, allow the pot to rest for about 12 minutes, and then use the quick release method to release the remainder of the pressure. When valve drops, carefully remove lid.

In a high-powered blender, blend the cashews with about two cups of the hot soup, until smooth and creamy. Return mixture to soup pot and stir well.

Add in navy beans, nutritional yeast, red pepper flakes, and fresh greens. Mix gently, and cover pot for 5 more minutes, or until greens are wilted and beans are heated through.

Garnish with fresh basil and serve hot.

STOVETOP

In a large soup pot, combine first 13 ingredients (onion through onion powder). Bring to boil.

Reduce heat, cover partially, and simmer gently, until the pasta is almost tender, approximately 10 minutes. Turn off the heat.

In a high-powered blender, blend the cashews with about two cups of the hot soup, until smooth and creamy. Return mixture to soup pot and stir well.

Add in navy beans, nutritional yeast, red pepper flakes, and fresh greens. Mix gently, and cover pot for 5 more minutes, or until greens are wilted and beans are heated through.

Garnish with fresh basil and serve hot.

Soup will be thicker and more stew-like with 10 ounces of uncooked pasta and have more broth with 6 ounces.

best split pea soup

Serves 8 to 10

My mom made a wonderful split pea soup when I was growing up, and this is my version, but of course without animal products or oil. We turn this soup into a hearty meal, adding diced potatoes, whole grain pasta and/or cooked greens to our bowls before ladling out all the bubbling goodness.

1 pound split peas, sorted and rinsed

2 quarts vegetable broth

1 large Vidalia onion, minced

1 or 2 cloves garlic, minced

2 or 3 stalks celery, chopped

2 or 3 carrots, finely chopped

2 bay leaves

2 teaspoons kosher salt (or to taste)

coarsely ground black pepper, to taste

SLOW COOKER

Combine all ingredients in a large slow cooker. Set to Low if using a newer slow cooker, or High if an older one, and cook for 7 to 9 hours, or until split peas are tender and soup becomes thick and creamy. Carefully remove bay leaves.

STOVETOP

Combine all ingredients in large soup pot and bring to a rolling boil. Cover and reduce heat, and continue simmering for around 2 hours, or until split peas are tender and soup becomes thick and creamy. Carefully remove bay leaves.

PRESSURE COOKER

Combine all ingredients in an electric pressure cooker.

Lock the lid in place. Select High Pressure and set the timer for 25 minutes.

After cooking is complete, allow the pot to rest for about 10 minutes, and then use the quick release method to release the remainder of the pressure. When valve drops, carefully remove lid. Carefully remove bay leaves.

For all methods, use an immersion blender to create an even creamier texture (if desired). Serving suggestion – wonderful over boiled potatoes, brown rice, whole grain pasta, or cooked greens.

winter stew with potatoes, barley, and lentils

Serves 10 to 12

This is a variation of an old northern European Jewish dish, called Cholent, that I developed by request for my father-in-law, years ago. I took liberties (originally) with the seasonings and eliminated the animal products, but otherwise have retained most of the traditional essence.

1 ½ quarts vegetable broth

1 large onion, diced

1 cup uncooked pearl barley, rinsed (not quick-cooking)

¾ cup uncooked brown or green lentils, sorted and rinsed

8 small potatoes, peeled, and cut into 1-inch or 1 ½-inch chunks

1 ½ cups chopped carrots

1 ½ cups chopped celery

2 cloves garlic, minced

3 to 4 tablespoons Bragg Liquid Aminos or soy sauce

1 teaspoon cumin

2 teaspoons kosher salt (or to taste)

¾ teaspoon coarsely ground black pepper (or to taste)

Combine all ingredients in large (6- or 7-quart) slow cooker. Cover and set to High for 7 hours, or until all vegetables are soft and tender. Season if needed with additional salt and pepper and serve hot.

ethiopian lentil soup

Serves 8 to 10

Berbere seasoning is an Ethiopian flavor combination (with paprika, red chile powder, chile flakes, fenugreek, ginger, cardamom, and cumin) that adds an exotic finish and elevates this soup from simple to outstanding.

1 large Vidalia onion, chopped

4 stalks celery, chopped

1 pound uncooked brown or green lentils, sorted and rinsed

6 cups vegetable broth

3 cups water

1 15-ounce can chopped or crushed tomatoes

1 15-ounce can tomato sauce (no sugar, no oil)

1 teaspoon Berbere seasoning

½ teaspoon cumin

2 teaspoons kosher salt (or to taste)

½ teaspoon coarsely ground black pepper

1 bay leaf

garnish: salt-free dry-roasted peanuts (optional)

STOVETOP

Combine all ingredients in a large soup pot.

Bring to boil. Once boiling, reduce heat to a simmer. Cover, and cook for one hour and 45 minutes, or until lentils are tender and begin to cook down to a smooth creamy soup.

Carefully remove the bay leaf. Use an immersion blender to create a slightly creamier texture (if desired).

Serve hot over brown rice, or along with toasted sprouted whole grain bread, or garnished with salt-free dry-roasted peanuts.

SLOW COOKER

Combine all ingredients in a large slow cooker.

Cover and cook on High setting for 6 to 8 hours or until lentils are tender. All slow cookers have their own personality – older ones may take longer. Newer ones may take less time.

Carefully remove the bay leaf. Use an immersion blender to create a slightly creamier texture (if desired).

Serve hot over brown rice, or along with toasted sprouted whole grain bread, or garnished with salt-free dry-roasted peanuts.

PRESSURE COOKER

Combine all ingredients in an electric pressure cooker.

Lock the lid in place. Select High Pressure and set the timer for 20 minutes.

After cooking is complete, allow the pot to rest for about 10 minutes, and then use the quick release method to release the remainder of the pressure. When valve drops, carefully remove lid.

Carefully remove the bay leaf. Use an immersion blender to create a slightly creamier texture (if desired).

Serve hot over brown rice, or along with toasted sprouted whole grain bread, or garnished with salt-free dry-roasted peanuts.

curried sweet potato, eggplant, and quinoa tagine

Serves 8

Tagines are savory North African stews usually prepared by slow cooking in a shallow cooking dish with a conical lid. This is my uncomplicated version, bursting with aromatic spices, colorful vegetables, and savory Moroccan flavor that tastes like it's been cooking all day.

1 onion, diced

1 clove garlic, minced

1 medium eggplant, peeled, and cubed in 1/2-inch pieces

1 medium or 2 small sweet potatoes, peeled, and cubed in 1/2-inch pieces

1 orange, yellow, or red bell pepper, diced in 1/2-inch pieces

1 cup uncooked quinoa

2 1/4 to 2 1/2 cups vegetable broth

1 15-ounce can black beans, rinsed and drained

1 1/2 teaspoons chili powder

1 teaspoon hot curry powder

2 teaspoons kosher salt (or to taste)

1/2 teaspoon coarsely ground black pepper

In a large electric pressure cooker, sauté the onion for a few minutes, using a little water to avoid sticking. Add garlic and stir for a few seconds, and then select Cancel to stop the sauté process.

Add the eggplant, sweet potatoes, bell pepper, quinoa, and broth. Stir in the black beans, and seasonings.

Lock the lid in place. Select High Pressure and set the timer for 5 minutes. After the cooking is complete, allow the pot to rest for about 10 minutes, and then use the quick release method to release the remainder of the pressure. When valve drops, carefully remove lid.

Serve hot over brown rice, or with sprouted whole grain tortillas.

cream of broccoli spinach soup

Serves 6 to 8

This soup is not only rich and comforting, but so satisfying served with baked potatoes or toasty sprouted whole grain bread. Use either fresh or frozen broccoli and toss in spinach at the end of the cooking time to boost the nutritional profile even more.

1 onion, diced

2 stalks celery, diced

2 large carrots, diced

1 to 2 cloves garlic, minced

½ red bell pepper, diced

2 medium potatoes, peeled, diced

5 cups chopped raw broccoli (or around 1 ¼ pounds frozen)

6 cups vegetable broth, divided

2 ½ teaspoons salt (or to taste)

½ teaspoon coarsely ground black pepper

dash of Cajun or Creole seasoning

1 cup raw cashews

1 cup fresh baby spinach, roughly chopped

garnish: fresh basil (optional)

STOVETOP

In a large soup pot over medium-high heat, sauté onions, celery, and carrots in about ¼ cup of water for about five minutes, or until soft and translucent.

Add garlic, bell pepper, and potatoes, and continue to cook for another couple of minutes.

Stir in 4 cups (only) of broth, the broccoli and seasonings. Bring to boil over high heat. Reduce heat to simmer, cover, and cook for about 20 minutes, or until potatoes and carrots are tender, stirring occasionally.

Using an immersion blender in the soup pot, create a mostly creamy soup to the desired texture.

Meanwhile, in a high-powered blender, blend the cashews with the last 2 cups of broth until smooth and creamy. Return mixture to soup pot and stir well.

Add spinach and allow the spinach to wilt from the heat.

Taste and add additional seasoning (if desired). Garnish (optional) with fresh basil and serve hot.

PRESSURE COOKER

In a large electric pressure cooker, sauté onions, celery, and carrots in about ½ cup of water for about five minutes, or until soft and translucent. Add more water as needed to prevent sticking.

Add garlic, bell pepper, and potatoes, and continue to sauté for another minute. Stop the sauté function and stir in 4 cups (only) of broth, the broccoli and seasonings.

Lock the lid in place. Select High Pressure for 5 minutes. After pressure cooking is complete, allow to rest for 4 minutes, then use the quick release method to release remainder of pressure. When valve drops, very carefully remove lid.

Using an immersion blender in the pot, create a mostly creamy soup to the desired texture.

Meanwhile, in a high-powered blender, blend the cashews with the last 2 cups of broth until smooth and creamy. Return mixture to soup pot and stir well.

Add spinach and allow the spinach to wilt from the heat.

Taste and add additional seasoning (if desired). Garnish (optional) with fresh basil and serve hot.

sweet endings

peanut butter and jelly cookies

Makes 24 cookies

Made with just five pantry ingredients, these are extra good, despite the simplicity. One batch makes two dozen cookies, and they freeze beautifully. In fact, they might be even better straight from the freezer.

½ cup natural peanut butter

¼ cup, plus 2 tablespoons peanut powder*

¾ cup fruit-sweetened strawberry jelly

¾ teaspoon baking soda

1 teaspoon pure vanilla extract

Preheat oven to 350 degrees.

In a large bowl, mix all ingredients until combined.

Scoop 1-inch balls of batter onto a baking sheet lined with either parchment paper or a silicone baking mat. Bake for 10 to 12 minutes, until tops feel close to firm.

Remove from oven and place pan on cooling rack. Enjoy warm or at room temperature. Extras freeze well too.

* Peanut powder is a single ingredient product, made only from peanuts, and can be found either online or at your local grocery store.

strawberry shortcake bars

Makes 24 to 30 (1 ½-inch) bars

*These are summery, sweet, moist, and tender, and will please
family and friends of every dietary persuasion.*

2 bananas

8 ounces, plus 4 ounces fresh
or frozen strawberries, divided
(if frozen, they should be slightly
thawed first)

¾ cup rolled oats

⅓ cup dates, pits removed

2 teaspoons baking powder

1 teaspoon pure vanilla extract

Preheat oven to 350 degrees.

Into the bowl of a food processor, add bananas, 8 ounces of strawberries, oats, dates, baking powder, and vanilla. Process until the mixture is well combined.

Remove bowl and blade from the base. Divide batter evenly, filling either a silicone brownie-bites pan or a nonstick miniature muffin pan. If you have more batter than fits easily, just start a second pan. You won't want to over-fill because these will rise a little bit.

Dice the remaining 4 ounces of strawberries, and dot them over the top of the batter, pressing just slightly so that they stay in place. Bake for 15 minutes, or until just firm.

Remove from oven and place on cooling rack. Allow to cool and enjoy.

chocolate peanut butter truffles

Makes 16 to 20 truffles

Richly flavored with cocoa and peanut butter, these truffles are sweetened only with dates, and are the perfect ending to a great meal when you want just a little bite of something very special.

TRUFFLES

1 cup dates, pits removed

½ cup natural peanut butter

3 tablespoons unsweetened cocoa or cacao powder

3 tablespoons peanut powder *

½ teaspoon vanilla bean powder (or 1 teaspoon pure vanilla extract)

pinch of salt (optional)

TRUFFLE COATINGS

¼ cup unsweetened cocoa or cacao powder

-OR-

¼ cup unsalted dry-roasted peanuts, finely chopped

In the bowl of a large food processor fitted with the metal blade, add dates, peanut butter, cocoa powder, peanut powder, vanilla, and salt (if using). Depending upon the moisture level of the dates, you may want to add a tablespoon or so of water to get the blade moving. Process until the mixture holds together well.

Once blended well, remove bowl and blade from the base. Line a baking sheet with parchment paper or silicone baking mat.

Using a small cookie scoop, a spoon, or clean hands, roll into 1-inch balls. The mixture may be a little sticky as you work. Place truffles on prepared baking sheet.

One by one, roll each truffle in a small dish of either cocoa powder or crushed peanuts.

Refrigerate or freeze truffles in an airtight container.

* Peanut powder is a single ingredient product, made only from peanuts, and can be found either online or at your local grocery store.

banana monkey bars

Makes approximately 24 (1 ½-inch) bars

The first batch I made of these disappeared before they even had a chance to cool. By the next morning, my husband, my son, and my daughter had each separately asked me to please make more.

3 bananas

¼ cup almond butter

¼ cup dates, pits removed

1 teaspoon pure vanilla extract

¾ cup rolled oats

2 teaspoons baking powder

Preheat oven to 350 degrees.

Into the bowl of a large food processor, add all ingredients in the order listed above. Process until the mixture is smooth and well combined.

Remove bowl and blade from the base. Divide batter evenly, filling either a silicone brownie-bites pan or a nonstick miniature muffin pan.

Bake for 14 minutes, or until tops are golden and firm to the touch. Remove from oven and place on cooling rack.

slow cooked baked apples

Serves 3

Here's my very simple, and barely sweet version of baked apples, utilizing the ease of gentle slow cooking; warm, fragrant spices; and just a touch of oats.

½ cup water

3 baking apples (Honeycrisp, Rome, or Pink Lady)

¼ cup rolled oats

1 teaspoon cinnamon

½ teaspoon apple pie spice

6 small dried apricots, diced

1 pitted Medjool date, diced

1 tablespoon date syrup

Pour the water into the bottom of a medium 3- to 4-quart slow cooker.

Wash and core the apples, taking care to avoid puncturing the base of the apples.

A melon baller or a teaspoon works well for this. Peel the top third of each apple. Set aside.

Into a small bowl, add the remainder of the ingredients (oats, spices, dried fruit, and date syrup), and combine very well. Stuff the apples evenly, using all of the filling mixture.

Carefully place the apples into the slow cooker. Cover and slow cook for about 60 to 75 minutes, on the Low setting for a newer slow cooker, or the High setting for an older one, or until the apples are almost tender. Don't overbake!

Serve warm.

chocolate blueberry brownies

Makes 18 to 24 (1 ½-inch) brownies

These brownies are studded with blueberries, and so fudgy good. They're perfect for creating a delicious excuse to celebrate anything, anytime.

---

2 bananas

1/2 cup rolled oats

1/2 cup unsweetened cocoa or cacao powder

1/4 cup dates, pits removed

2 teaspoons baking powder

1 teaspoon pure vanilla extract

1 1/4 cups fresh or frozen blueberries (if frozen, they do not need to be thawed first)

Preheat oven to 350 degrees.

Into the bowl of a food processor, add all ingredients, except the blueberries. Process until the mixture is well combined.

Remove bowl and blade from the base. Divide batter evenly, filling either a silicone brownie-bites pan or a nonstick miniature muffin pan.

Dot the berries over the top of the brownie batter, pressing just slightly so that they stay in place. Bake for 14 to 18 minutes, or until brownie tops are slightly firm.

Remove from oven and place on cooling rack. Allow to cool and enjoy.

apricot oatmeal cookies

Makes 30 to 35 cookies

These chewy cookies are high in fiber and delightfully simple. The pecans add crunch, and the fruit brings just the right balance to every bite.

2 ripe bananas

½ cup unsweetened applesauce

1 teaspoon pure vanilla extract

1 cup rolled oats

1 tablespoon ground flaxseed meal

1 teaspoon cinnamon

1 teaspoon baking powder

¼ cup pitted dates, chopped

¼ cup dried apricots, chopped

2 tablespoons raw pecans, chopped

2 tablespoons unsweetened coconut

Preheat oven to 350 degrees.

In a large bowl, mash bananas. Add applesauce and vanilla. To the banana mixture, add oats, flax, cinnamon, and baking powder. Combine well. Stir in dates, apricots, pecans, and coconut.

On a parchment paper lined baking sheet, drop rounded tablespoons of the batter. Flatten slightly with the back of a spoon.

Bake for 14 or 15 minutes, or until golden and firm to the touch. Remove from oven and allow to rest on a cooling rack briefly before serving.

raspberry-dusted cocoa date truffles

Makes 25 to 30 truffles

*Delight your favorite people with these little gems. Pure and
simple, yet holiday-worthy and decadently delicious.*

1 ¼ cups freeze-dried raspberries,
divided

1 ½ cups dates, pits removed

⅓ cup tahini

¼ cup unsweetened cocoa or cacao
powder

3 tablespoons raspberry liqueur,
brandy, or water

1 teaspoon pure vanilla extract

Using a food processor or a blender, process raspberries into a powder or simply place raspberries into zippered plastic bag, and manually crush with a rolling pin or kitchen mallet. Pour raspberry powder into a bowl and set aside.

In a large high-powered blender add ¼ cup (only) of the raspberries, plus the dates, tahini, cocoa or cacao powder, liqueur (or brandy or water), and vanilla, and process until smooth.

Turn power off, remove lid, and transfer blended mixture to a covered container. Freeze or refrigerate for an hour or more, or until mixture is well chilled.

Remove chilled mixture from refrigerator or freezer, scoop out small amounts, and roll into one-inch (or smaller) balls. Carefully roll one ball at a time in the remainder of the raspberry powder, covering each one completely. Repeat with remaining truffles.

Place truffles in an air-tight container and freeze to harden for 30 minutes or more before serving. Extras can be stored in the freezer for at least two weeks.

cinnamon applesauce donuts

Makes 9 donuts

We love these donuts so much. Soft and delicate, they're
outstanding with a cup of coffee, hot tea, or warm apple cider.

---

1 ¾ cups, plus 2 tablespoons rolled oats

1 ½ tablespoons baking powder

1 ½ teaspoons cinnamon

1 ½ cups dates, pits removed (tightly packed)

1 ½ cups water

¼ cup, plus 2 tablespoons nondairy milk, plain, unsweetened

½ cup unsweetened applesauce, plus extra cinnamon (to sprinkle over "frosted" donuts)

Preheat oven to 350 degrees. Have ready a silicone donut pan.

Add the oats to a high-powered blender, and briefly grind the oats into flour. Then turn power off, remove the lid, and add baking powder, cinnamon, dates, water, and milk. Process for a few moments to combine well.

Spoon the batter into a large plastic zippered storage bag, and seal to close. Cut a ½-inch opening in the corner of the bag with scissors, and carefully pipe batter into the donut pan. With the back of a spoon, smooth the tops of each one to make sure batter is evenly distributed.

Bake 12 to 16 minutes, or until donuts are firm on top to the touch. Allow to cool on a baking rack.

Just before serving, "frost" the tops of each donut, spreading about 1 tablespoon of applesauce over each donut. Sprinkle a dash of additional cinnamon over the layer of applesauce and enjoy.

peanut butter power balls

Makes 18 to 20 balls

These little power balls are great for a busy afternoon when you need a quick boost of energy. Add oats, peanut butter, and dried fruit to your food processor for an instant treat, with no baking required.

1 cup rolled oats

⅓ cup natural peanut butter

⅓ cup dried fruit (I like a mixture of apricots and dates)

¼ cup date syrup

2 tablespoons raw pecans

½ teaspoon cinnamon

pinch of salt (optional)

Add all ingredients to the bowl of a food processor. Process briefly, or pulse just a few times, until mixture begins to stick together, and is somewhat (but not entirely) blended.

Scoop small portions of the mixture out with a spoon. Roll into one-inch balls and enjoy, either chilled or at room temperature.

no-bake mocha brownies

Makes 24 (1 ½-inch) brownies

I adore all things mocha, so these brownies make me very happy. Perfect for a last minute very easy, very special dessert, and they freeze beautifully too.

2 cups raw walnuts

2 cups dates, pits removed

½ cup unsweetened cocoa or cacao powder

3 tablespoons prepared espresso (about 1 shot)

1 teaspoon pure vanilla extract

Place the walnuts in large food processor bowl, fitted with the metal blade. Process until ground to a fine powder.

Add dates, cocoa powder, espresso, and vanilla. Process until the mixture holds together well, which can take a few minutes. Depending upon the moisture level of the dates, you may want to add a tablespoon or so of water to get the blade moving. Process until the mixture holds together well.

Once well blended, remove bowl and blade from the base. Press the batter evenly into either 24 sections of a silicone brownie-bites pan or a nonstick miniature muffin pan. Cover and refrigerate for at least one hour before serving.

Store leftover brownies in refrigerator or freezer.

chocolate strawberry brownies

Makes 24 to 30 (1 ½-inch) brownies

*These amazing brownies are oh-so-fudgy good with the flavor
of cocoa and fresh strawberries in every bite.*

½ cup rolled oats

½ cup unsweetened cocoa or cacao powder

2 teaspoons baking powder

1 ripe banana

20 Medjool dates, pits removed

3 cups fresh strawberries (trimmed, rinsed, and patted dry), divided

2 teaspoons pure vanilla extract

Preheat oven to 375 degrees.

Into the bowl of a food processor, add oats, cocoa, and baking powder. Process for a few seconds. Add banana, dates, 2 cups (only) of the strawberries, and vanilla.

Process until the mixture is well combined.

Remove bowl and blade from the base. Divide batter evenly, filling either a silicone brownie-bites pan or a nonstick miniature muffin pan. I usually have enough batter to fill 30 sections, so I use 2 pans.

Dice the remaining 1 cup of berries. Dot the berries over the top of the brownie batter, pressing just slightly so that they stay in place. Bake for 15 to 20 minutes, or until firm.

Remove from oven and place on cooling rack. Allow to cool and enjoy.

apple cider sorbet

Makes approximately 1 quart

---

*One ingredient. Really. And absolutely the perfect way to finish a
lovely meal. No sugar added, and incredibly delicious.*

---

2 cups fresh apple cider

Carefully pour apple cider into the bowl of an automatic ice cream machine, and process according to manufacturer's instructions until desired texture is achieved.

Enjoy immediately or harden further in freezer for an hour or more.

sweet potato streusel bars

Makes 40 to 44 (1½-inch) bars

*These little gems have a sweet, crunchy sprinkle of streusel topping,
with the barest whisper of salt. They're so good that, seriously, no one
will guess you've left out sugar, oil, dairy, and eggs.*

SWEET POTATO BARS

1 medium or large sweet potato

2 ripe bananas

½ cup unsweetened applesauce

½ cup dates, pits removed

½ cup water

1 cup rolled oats

1 ½ teaspoons cinnamon

2 teaspoons baking powder

1 teaspoon pure vanilla extract

STREUSEL

½ cup dates, pits removed

¼ cup rolled oats

¼ cup raw pecans

¼ teaspoon cinnamon

pinch of salt (optional)

Scrub and pierce sweet potato, and microwave until tender. When cool enough to handle, remove skin. Measure 1 cup of cooked sweet potato (packed well) and set aside. Refrigerate any remaining sweet potato for another use.

Preheat oven to 350 degrees.

Into the bowl of a large food processor, add the measured 1 cup of sweet potatoes along with the other Sweet Potato Bar ingredients (bananas through vanilla). Process for a couple of minutes, until the mixture is very well combined. Remove bowl and blade from the base.

Divide batter evenly, filling a silicone brownie-bites pan or two. My pans hold 24 bars, so I use two pans.

Place the bowl and blade back on the base of the food processor. Add the Streusel ingredients and pulse several times to create the topping. Remove bowl and blade from the base.

Carefully top each bar with about ½ teaspoon of the streusel mixture. Pat in place very lightly. Bake for approximately 15 minutes, or until tops are golden and almost firm to the touch. Remove from oven and place on cooling rack.

mocha ice cream

Makes approximately 1 quart

Flavored with cocoa powder and shots of espresso, this ice cream is made with the purest of ingredients and sweetened only with dates.

1 cup prepared espresso (about 5 shots)

1 cup water

½ cup raw cashews

1 cup dates, pits removed

2 tablespoons unsweetened cocoa or cacao powder

1 teaspoon pure vanilla extract

pinch of salt (optional)

Add all ingredients to a high-powered blender and process until mixture is smooth and combined well.

Carefully pour mixture into the bowl of an automatic ice cream maker, and process according to manufacturer's instructions until desired texture is achieved.

Enjoy immediately or harden further in freezer for an hour or more.

mint chocolate brownies

Makes 16 to 20 (1 ½-inch) brownies

*These brownies are like chewy, delicious little miracles, and
so minty good. They freeze extremely well, too.*

1 cup dates, pits removed

½ cup unsweetened cocoa or cacao powder

1 tablespoon ground flaxseed meal

2 teaspoons baking powder

6 tablespoons unsweetened plain or vanilla almond milk

1 teaspoon pure peppermint extract

1 teaspoon pure vanilla extract

Preheat oven to 350 degrees.

In the bowl of a food processor, process the dates for a few seconds, and then add cocoa, flax, and baking powder, and process briefly. Add remainder of ingredients and process until the mixture is very well combined, stopping to scrape the side of the bowl, if needed. Remove bowl and blade from the base. Batter can be baked as either drop cookies or brownie bites.

DROP COOKIES

Roll batter into 1-inch balls. Place onto a baking sheet lined with either parchment paper or a silicone baking mat. Flatten batter slightly with the back of a spoon.

Bake for 14 to 18 minutes, or until almost firm. They will be more moist and fudgy with less baking time and become chewier when they bake longer.

Remove from oven and place on cooling rack. Allow to cool completely before removing from pan.

BROWNIE BITES

Divide batter evenly, filling a silicone brownie-bites pan.

Bake for 14 to 18 minutes, or until almost firm. They will be more moist and fudgy with less baking time and become chewier when they bake longer.

Remove from oven and place on cooling rack. Allow to cool completely before removing from pan. (Brownie bites may need a little careful coaxing out of the silicone pan with a small straight spatula.)

matcha green tea ice cream

Makes approximately 1 quart

Brimming with matcha green tea goodness, this frozen treat has immune boosters that may also help fight cancer, regulate blood sugar, and reduce the risk of heart disease.

1 ½ cups water

½ cup raw cashews

¾ cup dates, pits removed

3 teaspoons matcha green tea powder

1 teaspoon pure vanilla extract

Add all ingredients to a high-powered blender and process until mixture is smooth and combined well.

Carefully pour mixture into the bowl of an automatic ice cream maker, and process according to manufacturer's instructions until desired texture is achieved.

Enjoy immediately or harden further in freezer for an hour or more.

pineapple right-side-up cakes

Makes 24 to 30 (1 ½-inch) bars

These dessert bites are my version of Pineapple Upside Down Cake. Super easy with only six ingredients, they're moist and tender, and freeze well too.

2 bananas

1 cup, plus ½ cup fresh pineapple, divided

¾ cup rolled oats

⅓ cup dates, pits removed

2 teaspoons baking powder

1 teaspoon pure vanilla extract

Preheat oven to 350 degrees.

Into the bowl of a food processor, add bananas, 1 cup of pineapple, oats, dates, baking powder, and vanilla. Process until the mixture is well combined.

Remove bowl and blade from the base. Divide batter evenly, filling either a silicone brownie-bites pan or a nonstick miniature muffin pan. If you have more batter than fits easily, just start a second pan. You won't want to over-fill because these will rise.

Dice the remaining ½ cup of pineapple, and dot diced pineapple over the top of the batter, pressing just slightly so it stays in place. Bake for 15 to 18 minutes, or until almost firm.

Remove from oven and place on cooling rack. Allow to cool and enjoy.

peanut butter ice cream

Makes approximately 1 quart

Simple, creamy, and delicately sweet with just a hint of salt, your guests will never guess this frozen treat is dairy-free.

2 cups unsweetened plain or vanilla almond milk

1 ¼ cups dates, pits removed

¾ cup natural peanut butter

1 teaspoon pure vanilla extract

pinch of salt (optional)

Add all ingredients to a high-powered blender and process until mixture is smooth and combined well.

Carefully pour mixture into the bowl of an automatic ice cream maker, and process according to manufacturer's instructions until desired texture is achieved.

Enjoy immediately or harden further in freezer for an hour or more.

moroccan strawberry almond milkshake

Serves 1

Traditionally, Moroccan Almond Shakes are made with almonds and water, plus sugar or honey, and (often) orange blossom water. My lighter version (without sugar) turns pink and fruity with a splash of fresh strawberries.

4 ice cubes

3 to 5 Medjool dates, pits removed (use more or less, to taste)

½ cup unsweetened plain or vanilla almond milk

3 or 4 large strawberries (about one handful)

¼ banana

Place all ingredients in a high-powered blender.

Process first on low, and gradually work up to high speed until mixture is completely smooth. Pour into a glass and enjoy immediately.

more information

additional resources

*Among the many important resources from esteemed
pioneers in the field of whole food plant-based nutrition,
here are a few of my favorites:*

The Cheese Trap
NEAL D. BARNARD, M.D.
Physicians Committee for Responsible Medicine

Power Foods for the Brain
NEAL D. BARNARD, M.D.
Physicians Committee for Responsible Medicine

Dr. Neal Barnard's Program for Reversing Diabetes
NEAL D. BARNARD, M.D.
Physicians Committee for Responsible Medicine

The China Study
T. COLIN CAMPBELL, Ph.D. and THOMAS M. CAMPBELL, M.D.
T. Colin Campbell Center for Nutrition Studies

Whole
T. COLIN CAMPBELL, Ph.D.
T. Colin Campbell Center for Nutrition Studies

Prevent and Reverse Heart Disease
CALDWELL B. ESSELSTYN, JR., M.D.
Dr. Esselstyn's Program and Publications

How Not to Die
MICHAEL GREGER, M.D.
NutritionFacts.org

The Starch Solution
JOHN A. McDOUGALL, M.D. and MARY McDOUGALL
Dr. McDougall's Health and Medical Center

Forks Over Knives
ALONA PULDE, M.D. and MATTHEW LEDERMAN, M.D.
forksoverknives.com

The Forks Over Knives Plan
ALONA PULDE, M.D. and MATTHEW LEDERMAN, M.D.
forksoverknives.com

more books to support your journey

Unprocessed
CHEF AJ

The Secrets to Ultimate Weight Loss
CHEF AJ

Becoming Vegan
BRENDA DAVIS, R.D. and VESANTO MELINA, M.S., R.D.

The Good Karma Diet
VICTORIA MORAN

Main Street Vegan
VICTORIA MORAN

The Food Revolution
JOHN ROBBINS

The World Peace Diet
WILL TUTTLE

must-see films

What The Health

The Game Changers

Forks Over Knives

Cowspiracy

A Prayer for Compassion

recipe index

acknowledgments

So many remarkable people helped this project come to fruition.

I'm grateful to the plant-based pioneers who initially inspired my plant-based journey, including Dr. John McDougall, Dr. Caldwell Esselstyn, Dr. T. Colin Campbell, and Dr. Neal Barnard.

My deepest appreciation to Dr. Robert Breakey, for your leadership and commitment to community health, and for contributing such a thoughtful Foreword to this book.

I am extremely thankful to both Victoria Moran and Chef AJ, for your wisdom, advice, and professional examples. Your friendship means more than words can express.

Thank you to Jane Esselstyn, and thank you, Center for Nutrition Studies, for your immediate support of this project.

Thank you, Heather Dahman, for creative updates to my website when this book was still merely a twinkle in my eye.

A very special thank you to McArthur Binion and Modern Ancient Brown Inc. (modernancientbrown.com) for a development grant and your belief in this project from the very beginning.

Thank you, Thomas, at California Balsamic (californiabalsamic.com) for your enthusiastic project sponsorship.

Thank you, Colleen and Clarissa, at Date Lady (ilovedatelady.com) for your early support and confidence.

Thank you, Sara de le Hera and Zavor (zavoramerica.com) for your project support and collaborative partnership.

To my sister, Nancy, and brother, Peter, thank you for decades of love and encouragement.

To my husband, Steve, thank you for helping me find the time to create the space I needed to write this book, for bringing me hot coffee when I needed a break, and for being my tireless constant confidant, consultant, and number one fan.

To my daughter, Emily, and my son, Sam, you guys are the very best. Thank you for your patience, humor, and brilliant suggestions during hours of brainstorming over conceptual and visual decisions, big and small.

An extraordinary thank you to Marina Aris, my publisher, for your confidence in this book, your calm and masterful guidance, and for holding my hand through every phase along the way.

To each of my clients and students, you give meaning to this mission. Thank you for helping me discover new ways to help you be your best, and for inspiring me to create new recipes that meet specific dietary needs. I look forward so much to every opportunity we have to work together.

And finally, thank you, Ann Arbor Vegan Kitchen (annarborvegankitchen.com) blog readers. I treasure our connections, as well as your questions, comments, and feedback. You truly help bring my recipes to life, and I hope we will continue this journey together for many years to come.

about the author

Vicki Brett-Gach is a sugar-free, oil-free Certified Personal Chef, Whole Food Plant-Based Culinary Instructor, and Master-Certified Vegan Lifestyle Coach.

Vicki is Forks Over Knives Plant-Based Certified, and trained in Nutrition for a Healthy Heart, and in Dietary Therapy for Reversing Common Diseases. She holds certificates in Culinary Health Coaching, in Plant-Based Nutrition, and in Wellness Counseling.

As a coach, Vicki has helped people with health challenges across the nation reverse chronic conditions, one delicious meal at a time. She also provides corporate wellness counseling and teaches whole food plant-based cooking classes to individual clients and groups of all sizes.

Vicki has written articles and created original recipes for the T. Colin Campbell Center for Nutrition Studies website and served as a special project author for their updated Certificate in Plant-Based Nutrition Program with her "Plant-Based Food Guide: How to Eat Well on a Budget."

Her recipes have been featured in:
Barefoot Vegan, The Beet, Honest Cooking, The McDougall Newsletter
Center for Nutrition Studies Newsletter, The Vegan Friends Cookbook
Perfectly Plant-Based, The Main Street Vegan Academy Cookbook

education, training, and certifications

Main Street Vegan Academy
Master Vegan Lifestyle Coach and Educator
Certified Vegan Lifestyle Coach and Educator

Wellness Forum Health
Certified Personal Chef

Cornell University
Wellness Counseling Certificate

Harvard Medical School and the Institute of Lifestyle Medicine
Culinary Coaching Certificate

T. Colin Campbell Center for Nutrition Studies
Plant-Based Nutrition Certificate
Nutrition for a Healthy Heart Training

Rouxbe Culinary School
Forks Over Knives Plant-Based Certified

Dr. McDougall's Health and Medical Center
Starch Solution Certification
Dietary Therapy Training

WFPB.org
Whole Food Plant-Based Certified

Wayne State University
Master of Arts degree
Bachelor of Fine Arts degree

Ann Arbor Vegan Kitchen

WHOLE FOOD. PLANT-BASED. SIMPLE. HAPPY. DELICIOUS.

THANK YOU FOR READING

The Plant-Based for Life Cookbook
Deliciously Simple Recipes to Nourish, Comfort, Energize and Renew

If you enjoyed this book, please consider leaving
a short review on Goodreads or your website of choice.
Reviews help both readers and writers.
They are an easy way to support good work and help to
encourage the continued release of quality content.

Connect with Vicki Brett-Gach
annarborvegankitchen.com

Want the latest from the Brooklyn Writers Press?
Browse our complete catalog

brooklynwriterspress.com

Milton Keynes UK
Ingram Content Group UK Ltd.
UKHW020645121024
2117UKWH00011B/124

9 781952 991042